The Politics of Fantasy
C.S. Lewis and J.R.R. Tolkien

Studies in Speculative Fiction, No. 10

Robert Scholes, Series Editor

Alumni/Alumnae Professor of English and
Chairman, Department of English
Brown University

Other Titles in This Series

The Politics of Fantasy
C.S. Lewis and J.R.R. Tolkien

by
Lee D. Rossi

UMI RESEARCH PRESS

Ann Arbor, Michigan

The United Library
Garrett-Evangelical/Seabury-Western Seminaries
Evanston, IL 60201

Copyright © 1984
Lee D. Rossi
All rights reserved

Produced and distributed by
UMI Research Press
an imprint of
University Microfilms International
A Xerox Information Resources Company
Ann Arbor, Michigan 48106

Library of Congress Cataloging in Publication Data

Rossi, Lee D.
The politics of fantasy, C.S.Lewis and J.R.R.
Tolkien.

    (Studies in speculative fiction ; no. 10)
    Revision of thesis—Cornell University, 1972.
    Bibliography: p.
    Includes index.
    1. Fantastic fiction, English—History and criticism.
2. English fiction—20th century—History and criticism.
3. Lewis, C. S. (Clive Staples), 1898-1963—Political
and social views. 4. Tolkien, J. R. R. (John Ronald
Reuel), 1892-1973—Political and social views.
5. Social problems in literature. I. Title. II. Series.
PR888.F3R67 1984   823'.0876'09   84-16116
ISBN 0-8357-1597-3 (alk. paper)

The United Library
Garrett-Evangelical/Seabury-Western Seminaries
Evanston, IL 60201

PR 888
.F3R67
GESW

Contents

Acknowledgments

The author would like to acknowledge the help of Ms. Joanna Russ and Mr. Thomas D. Hill who read and commented on this work during its composition. He would also like to thank Mr. Jonathan Bishop for his thoughtful suggestions and unflagging interest in the project. Finally, he would like to thank James and Carolyn Scott, whose intelligent enthusiasm for fantasy first stirred his own interest in these writers and their work.

Preface

C.S. Lewis and J.R.R. Tolkien are two of the most interesting and entertaining writers of fantasy in the twentieth century. Certainly they are two of the most popular, and in their own domain, they have been considered among the very best of modern practitioners. The literary and artistic merits of their work are in themselves enough to justify an extended discussion of their work.

But they have another interest for the student of intellectual and cultural history. They present striking examples of the moral dilemma with which all conscientious intellectuals must deal. Not out of society but unhappy in it, they are among many who have attempted a mode of escape and criticism of modern society. They have been among the most sensitive registers of the moral crisis in modern capitalist society.

As Christians steeped in the doctrine of original sin, of course, they see no possibility of any kind of radical improvement by the unaided action of the human will, and Lewis, in particular, seems to have a positive horror of revolutionary leftism as hopelessly philistine, and in extremity wicked. Their imaginative interests lie almost exclusively elsewhere. Tolkien's best work is an expression of a profound pessimism about human nature and political society, a pessimism formed by the debacle of World War I in which so many of Tolkien's generation fought and died. Lewis's best work involves a withdrawal from politics into a concern for the ethical life of the individual and an attempt to create alternative worlds where one might escape the evils of the modern world. Their practical concern for Christianity connects with these imaginative concerns insofar as it provides a future refuge from modern society, as well as an ethical stance from which to criticize it.

Both men are also, of course, well known—and deservedly so—as literary scholars, but their work in this area is touched on only as it reflects the imaginative concerns of their stories. Lewis, moreover, has written a tremendous amount of purely apologetic material—lectures, sermons, radio talks, and book-length works of popular theology. Though having their own interest, they have been thoroughly picked over in a number of books on Lewis's theology. For my own part, I find them the least interesting part of his work. Not that they don't usually display intelligence, wit, and an affability unusual in theological writing. But it is only in his novels that he overcomes the facile dialectician in his personality and allows the deepest level of his sensibility to speak. It is only at such times that he is able to produce works of lasting interest.

1

Tolkien and Lewis: The Literature of Political Despair

*I have claimed that Escape is one of the main functions of fairy-
stories, and since I do not disapprove of them, it is plain that I do
not accept the tone of scorn or pity with which "Escape" is now
so often used.... In using Escape in this way the critics have
chosen the wrong word, and, what is more, they are confusing,
not always by sincere error, the Escape of the Prisoner with the
Flight of the Deserter.... [They] stick their label of scorn not
only on to Desertion, but on to real Escape, and what are often
its companions, Disgust, Anger, Condemnation, and
Revolt.... Escapism has another and even wickeder face:
Reaction.*

J.R.R. Tolkien, "On Fairy-Stories"

*There is a grain of seriousness in my sally against the Civil
Service. I don't think you have worse taste or worse hearts than
other men. But I do think the State is increasingly tyrannical and
you, inevitably, are among the instruments of that tyranny.*

C.S. Lewis, Letter to I.O. Evans

Fantasy, as C.S. Lewis rightly points out, has been with us since men first began
to tell stories.[1] Ghosts, wizards, giants, and talking animals are as old as the
human imagination. In the last three centuries, however, with the development
of the novel the value of this kind of literature has been seriously questioned,
and its fantastic elements relegated to stories for children. It is only when they
are looking to be amused that adults resort to this literature at all. Serious
literature, complains Lewis, means realism and only realism. This rise of a
realistic aesthetic has impoverished our response to literature; it has left
modern audiences unprepared for and unreceptive to the wonders and beauties
of this earlier literature.

J.R.R. Tolkien, a friend of Lewis and like him a don at Oxford for many years, also takes a serious interest in this older literary form.[2] In fact, he is if anything more assertive in pressing its claim. It is not just that its antiquity and its beauties make it worthy of our attention; for Tolkien, fantasy is the highest power of the human imagination. He coins the word "sub-creation" to express this power. By means of it, the fantasist creates a whole imaginative world, a world with its own climate, geography, peoples, and languages. It is a power not unlike the divine power of primary creation; it signifies that man is made in the image of God.

As this last point suggests, Lewis's and Tolkien's attachment to fantasy implies a grand scheme of cultural reclamation. Tolkien and Lewis are two of the more recent heirs of a long tradition of culturally reactionary fantasists that goes back at least to Scott and includes such figures as George MacDonald, John Ruskin, William Morris, Lord Dunsany, and E.R. Eddison. Taken together, these writers constitute a cultural rearguard of the Middle Ages. Like MacDonald and others in this tradition, Tolkien and Lewis attach tremendous importance to the Christian faith and a traditional church. Like many of these writers, they exhibit a tremendous nostalgia for the political stability and cultural cohesion of the Middle Ages. Most importantly, they exhibit, as do these earlier writers, a version of the pastoral reflex. Like their nineteenth-century predecessors, Tolkien and Lewis react vigorously against the ugliness and squalor of modern industrialism. Both Lewis's Narnia and Tolkien's Shire present highly idealized landscapes unscarred by modern commerce and industry.

Of course, we must not minimize the areas of difference between this Christian and antimechanical critique of modern society and other brands of radicalism. Where others want to change or overturn existing social and political relations immediately, Tolkien and Lewis ultimately want to withdraw completely from politics. Where others would use the machines for more humane purposes, they would presumably get rid of most of the machines and return to a predominantly agricultural economy. Nevertheless, it would be helpful at the beginning of this paper to emphasize their distance from their contemporary surroundings and their alienation from the dominant trends of capitalist society. Thus in describing their politics, which is a major concern of this paper, we cannot remain satisfied with easy labels of "conservative" or "rightist." That they appear conservative today is, I believe, due mainly to the fact that they did not see any alternative to the present situation which wasn't potentially worse. We should remember too that their's is not a programmatic or virulent form of conservatism. Compared with such staunch right-wing Catholics as Maritain or Berdyaev, these men appear particularly mild. It would be fairer to say of them that, as far as practical politics are concerned, they are basically apolitical. In both the quotations which open this chapter, we notice a profound distaste for political society. Tolkien, for example, is primarily interested in escaping from politics. And we sense that the "Disgust, Anger, Condemnation and Revolt"—a remarkable and passionate collocation of words—of which he speaks, are really his own reaction to the immediate political prospect. Lewis, of course, is the more complicated case. But whatever the uses to which his statements on morals may be put by the establishment, at the subjective level Lewis is convinced that his work must remain "above" politics to be effective. Coupled with this is the attitude, especially pronounced toward the end of his life, that "Government is at best a necessary evil"(*L,* 281).

There is an element, then, to the "reaction" announced by Tolkien and practiced by them both which is similar to the critical project of other radicals, and that is its felt distance from contemporary society. The recurring element in their statements about their place in society is a distaste for the cultural, political, and above all, moral level of modern society. Tolkien, for example, calls Oxford, "an oasis of sanity in a desert of unreason" (*TR,* 62). Thus "reaction," in this sense, is not to be identified with "law and order" or with an attack on the working class, as in the Nixon version. Instead it desires a transformation of society as great as that envisioned by Marx, and while the outlines of that transformation are vague, the animus behind it is not. Though we feel the spirit of Arnold lurking in the background of this quotation from Lewis, its polemical energy is all Lewis's:

> "Democracy" or the "democratic spirit" (diabolical sense) leads to a nation without great men, a nation mainly of sub-literates, full of cocksureness which flattery breeds on ignorance, and quick to snarl or whimper at the first hint of criticism.

In place of "democracy" Lewis would have a society where "talent is placed in high posts, and where the ignorant mass are allowed no say at all in public affairs" (*SL,* 169).

This alienation is undoubtedly reflected in their choice of literary genres. Lewis uses the science-fiction and fairy tale genres not only because they are good vehicles for satire but also because they are excellent vehicles for escape from modern society. As Lewis says, "In life and art both we are always trying to catch in our net of successive moments something that is not successive" (*OOW,* 38), something that is not in time, in history, in politics, but out of them all together. Tolkien finds in fantasy a vehicle which will capture the profound evils which he sees in our social life. As he says in his essay "On Fairy-Stories," his interest in fantasy was "quickened to life by war." Just as the *Beowulf* author needed a dragon to personify fully the evils of his world (see Tolkien's essay, "*Beowulf:* the Monster and the Critics"), so Tolkien's fairy tale monsters are "personifications of malice, greed, and destruction" (*TR,* 42) equal to the times. Thus although "escape" is a very important word in Tolkien's theorizing about the genre in which he works, his own work is not "escapist" in the least. It confronts precisely those problems of politics and public morality which so harassed his own generation. Concerning an episode late in *The Lord of the Rings,* in which the mild pastoral countryside of the Shire endures the ravages of an industrial economy, he says, "It has indeed some basis in experience, though slender (for the economic situation was entirely different), and much further back [than the time when he was finishing the tale, i.e. 1952–53]. The country in which I lived in childhood was being shabbily destroyed before I was ten, in days when motor-cars were rare objects (I had never seen one) and men were still building suburban railways" (*FR,* xii).

For both writers, then, the motive for fantasy is essentially an attempt to liberate themselves from the ugliness and moral impasse of the modern world. Thus involved in this "fantasy" literature and this "escapist" genre is the total character of bourgeois society as it developed up to and beyond the First World War.

It is in reaction to this experience that they generate an ideology which expresses and legitimates their alienation. It is a reaction not unlike that of the "lost generation" of Hemingway, which came out of the war with all idols shattered and all ambition lost. Tolkien and Lewis espouse a social and cultural order which they feel to be untainted by the society responsible for the present holocaust. We must realize of course that this "reaction" is, by its very nature, theoretical and not practical. Implicit in Christian theology, but buttressed by these writers' experience of political society (especially their experience in the war), is the conviction that human society can never really progress, that political activity is meaningless and best left alone. These Christian reactionaries have no political program. They find no social group which responds spontaneously to their ideology and which could carry through their program of cultural reform. They feel isolated not only from the bourgeois and the working class, but also from their peers in the intelligentsia, a group which is itself becoming increasingly secular. Lewis's public activity is limited to appeals to the consciences of private individuals.

To discover how they arrived at this extreme of isolation is to trace the spiritual biography of at least one part, one very articulate and sensitive part, of the generation which came of age with the First World War. For both Tolkien and Lewis the war was undoubtedly a crucial experience. Both of them were junior officers in the front line at a time when the average life expectancy for junior officers was twenty days. All but one of Tolkien's close friends was killed in the war. After some six months in the line, Lewis was badly wounded when a shell from an English battery fell short. Tolkien's horror of war is evident not just in his description of the war-torn landscape of Mordor but also in this unusual personal revelation: "One has indeed personally to come under the shadow of war to feel fully its oppression but as the years go by it seems now often forgotten that to be caught in youth by 1914 was no less hideous an experience than to be involved in 1939 and the following years. By 1918 all but one of my close friends were dead" (*FR*, xi). Lewis shares much the same feeling, but he is unwilling to say very much about it, about the fighting that is. He can regale us with stories about the good comradeship, the good conversation, and the books he managed to read,

> But for the rest, the war—the frights, the cold, the smell of H.E., the horribly smashed men still moving like half-crushed beetles, the sitting or standing corpses, the landscape of sheer earth without a blade of grass, the boots worn day and night till they seemed to grow to your feet—all this shows rarely and faintly in memory. It is too cut off from the rest of my experience and often seems to have happened to someone else. It is even in a way unimportant. One imaginative moment seems now to matter more than the realities that followed. (*SbJ*, 196)

The interesting thing about this passage is that the description of the horrors of the war are much more vivid than the "imaginative moments" for which he opts. This is offset to an extent by the many pages in which he has carefully and lovingly related those moments. But the vividness of the images of war suggests the power which these memories and that experience still have over him.

Despite the fact that the war is so important for both of them, this importance is expressed in their fantasy in very different ways. In his best known and most important work, *The Lord of the Rings,* Tolkien's fantasy deals with a public world very much like Europe of the early twentieth century, a world in which struggle and violence are recurring realities. For fifteen hundred pages we are poised on the brink of terrible cataclysm which threatens to destroy all that is good in the world. For Tolkien power is the central issue. But the issue turns on whether his hero can or will destroy the ring of power. Thus it is not simply a matter of good overcoming evil. Within the good themselves lurks the lust for power, and the only thing that can check this lust is the absence of the tools of power. Thus the ring, which is the ultimate such tool, must be destroyed. This is the solution of a sensibility which, as we have seen, is profoundly distressed by the violence of modern technology. It mirrors Tolkien's horror at the misuse of political and social power in this century.

Given this quotient of public violence, Lewis's fantasy takes up the task of finding some alternative systems of value which will compensate the private man. The war, however, only confirmed a tendency, already present in Lewis's personality, to withdraw from society into a private world of fantasy and art. The crucial factors in forming these early romantic attitudes were his experiences with his father, a successful but unsympathetic man, and with his public school and its frantic and vicious social life, which always remained for Lewis an incarnation of The World. Lewis began writing fantasy as a child, but it was of a totally different character from his later work. His childish stories were acts of imaginative sympathy with the political and social world inhabited by his father. But as an adult writer, Lewis creates worlds radically alternative to the one in which he and his readers live. Lewis's Mars, Venus, and Narnia embody all those elements of magic, anarchy, and adventure, of natural beauty and delight which the real world lacks or lacks in the desired abundance. It is an avowedly fictive world in which all the desires and ambitions frustrated by the real world may be satisfied. Lewis, of course, realizes that these satisfactions are only imagined and not to be placed beside real satisfactions. Yet the things which he makes us see most clearly, the domestic relations of his child-heroes, the beauty and wonder of his imaginative landscapes, the quirky and sometimes terrifying vividness of his talking animals and other supporting characters are as wonderful as any literary experiences could be. Curiously, though questioning the fantasy principle, these books do not lead us back to the real world (as in *The Wizard of Oz*). Nor are they content to let us rest in the limited though real satisfactions of the imagined world. Rather they lead us away from it into a shadowy Narnia beyond Narnia, the metaphysical ground of all goodness. One wonders how Lewis could expect his readers to accept this. This heaven toward which Narnia is supposed to point doesn't have nearly as much imaginative validity as the imagined world itself. We sense that Lewis is not really being honest with us or even with himself. But this dishonesty is not dishonorable, merely an index of his conviction that there is no ultimate satisfaction in returning to the real world.

Lewis and Tolkien are symptomatic, then, of a condition which affects a whole generation. They are put a question by their history, perhaps the hardest which any generation has had to deal with. That these particular individuals failed to achieve a "realistic" answer is not so much a matter of their own personal failure as of the difficulty of the situation.

2

"Logic" and "Romance": The Divided Self of C.S. Lewis

In an essay on "C.S. Lewis: The Man and the Mystery," Chad Walsh, an Episcopalian priest and author of *C.S. Lewis: Apostle to the Skeptics,* notes that "the mystery of C.S. Lewis is that there seems to be no mystery. None, at least, if one views the man through his books."[1] Clyde Kilby, a personal friend of Lewis and the author of *The Christian World of C.S. Lewis,* remarks similarly but in a more personal vein, "My impression is that few people ever faced the delusive nature of selfishness more thoroughly than Lewis.... What his detractors do not understand—or maybe what they understand only too well—is that Lewis had come out on the other side of a door most of us never manage to enter."[2] Likewise, another friend, Austin Farrer, observes that Lewis's apologetic writings "express a solid confidence." He calls Lewis "a bonny fighter" and observes that, "From temper...he loved an argument."[3] What most impresses these writers—and they are representative of the majority opinion—is Lewis's stability of character and purpose. He is one of the very few authors of the twentieth century to whom individuals in spiritual turmoil turn again and again for consolation and guidance. There is hardly a memoir in the volume, *These Found the Way; Thirteen Converts to Protestant Christianity,* in which Lewis is not mentioned as one of the authors responsible for bringing the individual to Christianity. He figures, for instance, in the conversion narratives of such different individuals as Chad Walsh, an American Southerner who, in reacting to the narrowness of his upbringing, became an atheist; Hyatt Howe Waggoner, a university professor noted for his writings on American literature; and William Lindsay Gresham, a writer and a Communist veteran of the Spanish Civil War. Most striking of all is the narrative written by Gresham's wife, Joy Davidman. A poet and an editor of the Communist periodical, *The New Masses,* she tells how she had reached a crucial moment in her life, her faith in the Communist Party shattered, her marriage dissolving, her husband an alcoholic. She was without any belief to guide her life. At the very worst moment, she says that she experienced the presence of God. In solemn testimony to Lewis's helpfulness, she says that after that experience she started reading Lewis and "learned from him, slowly, how I had gone wrong. Without his works, I wonder if I and many others might not still be infants 'crying in the night.'"[4] She recounts that later she and her husband were reconciled and that, after an intensive study of Christian writers (Lewis, in particular), they both converted to Christianity.[5]

For many readers and critics, then, Lewis has an enviable sureness about the nature of the universe and his place in it. He is a spiritual father for those who like Joy Davidman are "infants crying in the night." Yet, for many other readers, Lewis's almost pugnacious certitude betrays a lack of appreciation for the complexities of the spiritual life. His friend and Oxford colleague, Nevill Coghill, observes that "Underneath all, I sense in his style an indefeasible core of Protestant certainties . . . but the strength that [he] derive[s] from this hard core deprived him of certain kinds of sympathy and perception."[6]

Chad Walsh, elaborating on this point, declares that Lewis paid a price for his conviction "that in the Christian faith there is available the essential things one needs to know in order to be a proper part of the totality." He observes that just as his religious thinking is somewhat shrill and moralistic, so too his literary judgments are a little too clearcut and simplistic. These habits of mind infect his creative work as well. Whereas Lewis is capable of creating characters who are "vivid and believable," they evince the same mysterious quality that one finds in Lewis himself. Says Walsh, "After he presents them to a certain depth, the curtain descends, and the reader is not sure whether anything exists behind."[7] For Walsh, the basic limitation of Lewis's thought is its lack of spiritual depth, and he relates this to Lewis's complete lack of interest in his own psychology. But ultimately he finds "Lewis's total absorption in the world outside himself" refreshing and healthy in an age full of "Ego-searching and Id-probing."

Still other readers find the key to Lewis's personality in the depths that Lewis leaves unexplored. In the introduction to *Light on C.S. Lewis,* a volume of memoirs and essays, Lewis's very close friend, Owen Barfield, observes that there was a peculiar enigmatic quality to Lewis's literary personality. Incapable of writing in the idiom of his own time, Lewis was nevertheless capable of breathing life into the motifs of the literary past. And yet there was something curiously forced, not insincere but unnatural, about this bravura performance.[8] The problem for Barfield lies in deciding what is depth and what surface, what is real and what is the product of the will. He feels that there is more to Lewis than the forceful and pugnacious apologist for Christianity. In fact, as time went on he came to feel more and more strongly that there were actually two Lewises. One was the shy and friendly student he had known at Oxford after the war, an uncertain young man hovering between rationalism and romanticism. The other developed after Lewis's conversion to

Christianity. This new Lewis had put all his force of will and skill as a dialectician to work on behalf of Christianity. "There was both a friend and the memory of a friend; sometimes they were close together and nearly coalesced; sometimes they seemed very far apart."[9]

As Barfield indicates, there seems to have been a basic duality in Lewis's personality. As a corollary, we might see some basic distinction between Lewis's apologetic and religious discourse, the work of the "new" Lewis, and his works of fantasy, the work of the "old" Lewis. This view contradicts the usual judgment about the place of Lewis's fantasy in his total career. Following Lewis's account in his autobiography, most of the critics see in his conversion a resolution of the tension, which Lewis had felt as a young man, between romanticism and rationalism. As Walsh says, "The two strands that run through C.S. Lewis's books are 'logic' and 'romance,' to give them the names he chose. Jointly they led him back to Christianity."[10] Moreover, most writers on Lewis hold that Lewis's fantasy is merely another mode of a basically apologetic activity. Richard Cunningham presents the usual view when he remarks, "In the case of C.S. Lewis, his apologetic method is inseparable from its literary vehicle; the Logos (something said) is intimately bound up with Poiema (something made)."[11] Others, notably Walsh and Kilby, spend a great deal of time elucidating the Christian content of Lewis's fantasies.

Yet the evidence, both literary and biographical, strongly suggests some kind of duality in his work. Lewis's fiction, for example, oscillates between two poles—the satire predominant in *The Screwtape Letters* and *That Hideous Strength* and the "marvellous" landscapes and characters of *Out of the Silent Planet, Perelandra,* and the Narnia books. Of the two, satire is obviously the genre most closely related to the ends of Christian apologetics. It assumes, as the critical focus, the morality and world view of Christianity. The imaginary landscape presupposes no such underpinning. It can be enjoyed for its own sake. Perhaps this is why the Christian writers who have dealt with Lewis's work have been so anxious to point out the moral of his so-called mythic fantasies. The kind of wonder and joy which they evoke and which originally attracted Lewis to "marvellous literature" are as far removed from the prescriptions of Christianity as they are from the realities of everyday life.

Secondly, the tone of Lewis's fiction involves the same kind of polarities. His satires are serious, sober-minded affairs; their humor, if any, mordant. The Lewis of the fairy tales, on the other hand, is unquestionably ebullient. He expresses real joy in the company of his Narnian characters and in their surroundings. Yet this joy is not a result of their conformance to Christian morality but rather of the freedom and magic of the imaginary world.

Finally, the uses of language oscillate between two poles. We might call them the rational and the romantic, or the didactic and the playful. Here is an example from his imaginary voyage to Mars, *Out of the Silent Planet*; a

Martian creature is trying to explain to the hero Ransom the nature of "eldils" (angels):

> Body is movement. If it is at one speed, you smell something; if at another, you hear a sound; if at another you see a sight; if at another, you neither see nor hear nor smell, nor know the body in any way. But mark this, Small One, that the two ends meet. If movement is faster, then that which moves is more nearly in two places at once. But if the movement were faster still—it is difficult, for you do not know many words—you see that if you made it faster and faster, in the end the moving thing would be in all places at once, Small One. Well, then, that is the thing at the top of all bodies—so fast that it is at rest, so truly body that it has ceased being body at all. But we will not talk of that. Start from where we are, Small One. The swiftest thing that touches our senses is light. We do not truly see light, we only see slower things lit by it, so that for us light is on the edge—the last thing we know before things become too swift for us. But the body of an *eldil* is a movement swift as light; you may say its body is made of light, but not of that which is light for the *eldil*. His "light" is a swifter movement which for us is nothing at all; and what we call light is for him a thing like water, a visible thing, a thing he can touch and bathe in—even a dark thing when not illumined by the swifter. And what we call firm things—flesh and earth—seem to him thinner, and harder to see, than our light, and more like clouds, and nearly nothing. To us the *eldil* is a thin, half-real body that can go through walls and rocks: to himself he goes through them because he is solid and firm and they are like cloud. And what is true light to him and fills the heaven, so that he will plunge into the rays of the sun to refresh himself from it, is to us the black nothing in the sky at night. (*OSP,* 94–95)

Clearly we have here two kinds of discourse. One is a definition, the other a hypothesis, a metaphor; one is abstract and the other concrete. The first is discursive and proceeds by a logical progression. The argument starts at one kind of speed which is available to our senses and progresses until the speed outstrips our senses. Ultimately, the only recourse of the argument is speculation, the only language paradox. But notice that with the repeated "Small One" Lewis is trying to give his speaker an authority which his argument doesn't have of itself. Obviously this kind of discourse is unsatisfactory, if not from a doctrinal point of view at least from a literary one. The Martian has to start again "from where we are." The vocabulary becomes more concrete, the syntax less authoritative. And the Martian is able to satisfy Ransom's curiosity. It is a moment of imaginative clarity, in which a possible other world is suggested in all its ramifications. We see side by side in this example what we see in various mixtures in Lewis's other fiction: a kind of language which emphasizes logic (as in his polemical works) and a language which is more playful and concrete.

    Those who have written about Lewis have not been wrong in appraising the virtues of his writing.[12] There is general agreement that he is at his best when creating imaginary worlds full of wonder and whimsy. But they have not noticed that these virtues are not a direct result of his commitment as a Christian. Instead his fantasy expresses an impulse much older than his

Christianity, the romanticism which, as John Lawlor points out, can never find a permanent home in the clearly structured logical world of medieval Christianity. Lawlor, a student of Lewis during the thirties, observes that Lewis's "emergent romanticism challenges religion as the revelation of final reality.... The myth... flies at the touch of a colder religion."[13]

At the bottom of this romanticism we find a pattern basic to Lewis's temperament, the escape into an imaginary world. The other touchstones of Lewis's imagination, the love of inanimate nature and the consolation of a small circle of friends, are variations on this basic theme of escape. Moreover, we may turn the critical cliche around and say that it is not so much that Lewis's fantasy is an aspect of his Christian commitment, as that his Christianity is an aspect of his commitment to fantasy. Both are evidence of his profound desire for a reality alternative to modern bourgeois society. And, as we shall see, this desire is grounded in Lewis's experience as a child and a young man.

C.S. Lewis was born in Belfast, in Protestant Ireland, in 1898. He was the son of a well-to-do solicitor. His father belonged to the first generation of professionals in a family of Welsh farmers. His mother was the daughter of a naval chaplain, and the descendant of clergymen, lawyers, and sailors. He tells us that his father was an extremely emotional man with a strong love of rhetoric; he was by far the dominant figure in the family. His mother was a much less powerful presence, but Lewis remembers her for her cheerfulness and quiet affection. Both parents were bookish people, and instilled their love for literature in both their sons.

The two most important things about this early period of Lewis's life was his inability to get along with his father, and the death of his mother before he was ten. His father was an aggressive and domineering person who took little cognizance of the people around him. At times this was not without its comical aspects. "Tell him that a boy called Churchwood had caught a fieldmouse and kept it as a pet, and a year, or ten years later, he would ask you. 'Did you ever hear what became of poor Chickweed who was so afraid of the rats?' For his own version, once adopted, was indelible, and attempts to correct it only produced an incredulous, 'Hm! Well, that's not the story you *used* to tell'" (*SbJ*, 13–14). In general, however, his inability to really listen to other people completely frustrated all attempts at communication. Of his mother's death Lewis says that "all settled happiness, all that was tranquil and reliable, disappeared from my life. There was to be much fun, many pleasures, many stabs of Joy; but no more of the old security. It was sea and islands now; the great continent had sunk like Atlantis" (*SbJ*, 21). The last sentence, especially, is extraordinarily intense and reflects the extent to which his mother's presence guaranteed his own emotional stability. Moreover, the effect of his wife's death was to make Lewis's father harsher and more demanding of his sons at a time when they most needed sympathy and guidance. "Under the pressure of anxiety his temper became incalculable; he spoke wildly and acted unjustly. Thus by a peculiar cruelty of fate, during those months the unfortunate man, had he but known it, was really losing his sons as well as his wife" (*SbJ*, 19). Nor did the gap between father and sons ever really close. In 1916 Lewis was preparing for a scholarship examination at Oxford. But faced with the imminent necessity of going into the army, he was losing interest in preparing for the exam. "I once tried," writes Lewis, "to explain this to my father; it was one of attempts I often made . . . to break through the artificiality of our intercourse and admit him to my real life. It was a total failure" (*SbJ*, 183). The elder Lewis could only respond with platitudes and homilies.

As a result of this thoroughly unsatisfactory relationship, Lewis and his brother were thrown completely on their own resources. The extent to which this alienation from his father provoked feelings of sadness and disappointment is evident in Lewis's remark that he and his brother "drew daily closer together . . . two frightened urchins huddled for warmth in a bleak world" (*SbJ*, 19).

This tendency to view the world in terms of a small group huddled together against a threatening reality was reinforced by Lewis's disastrous experience at his first school. His brother was already there, and Lewis was sent at age ten. The master—called Oldie by his victims—was cruel and the work pure drudgery. This experience of a cruel and tedious schoolmaster repeated the pattern set at home, and Lewis responded by banding together with his classmates in opposition to the master, much as he had drawn closer to his brother at home. Lewis suggests that these two experiences had an indelible, formative effect on his personality. He writes, "To this day the vision of the world which comes most naturally to me is one in which 'we two' or 'we few' (and in a sense 'we happy few') stand together against something stronger and larger" (*SbJ*, 32). Moreover, his experience with his father's horrible temper was repeated when Oldie, at the death of his own wife, became even more cruel and violent. "You will remember that I had already learned to fear and hate emotion," Lewis tells us. "Here was fresh reason to do so" (*SbJ*, 33).

But these experiences, crucial as they were, only served to confirm a reticence that seems certainly the result of a leisurely if isolated bourgeois way of life. From his earliest moments, Lewis's most intense experiences seem to have been primarily imaginative. The "New House" in the suburbs of Belfast, which his family moved into in the summer of 1905, is an extremely important factor in Lewis's development. "I am a product of long corridors, empty sunlit rooms, upstairs indoor silences, attics explored in solitude, distant noises of gurgling cisterns and pipes, and the noise of wind under tiles" (*SbJ*, 10). This sense of isolation was further increased by the departure of his older brother to school. We can see that eventually this solitude became a matter of choice and of habit rather than a matter of necessity. It was at this time, when Lewis first learned to read and write, that he began drawing and composing stories. "I soon staked out a claim to one of the attics and made it 'my study.' Pictures, of my own making or cut from the brightly colored Christmas numbers of magazines, were nailed on the walls. There I kept my pen and inkpot and writing books and paintbox; and there: Than to enjoy delight with liberty? What more felicity can fall to creature" (*SbJ*, 12–13). This recourse to art and literature (and not to more ordinary boyhood pursuits) was necessitated by a physical defect both sons inherited from their father. Each had only one joint in the thumb and were consequently disqualified from every kind of activity involving manual skill. Lewis remembers compulsory games at school as being some of the most dreadful times in his life. But Lewis seems always to have been a person who could make a virtue of necessity, and devoted great energy to the creation and elaboration of his private world, even to making a map and a history separate from the stories. "At this time—at the age of six, seven, and eight—I was living almost entirely in my imagination; or at least the imaginative experience of those years now seems to me more important than anything else" (*SbJ*, 15).

This imaginary world was called Boxen, and it was very different from Lewis's adult stories. (For a complete description of this work, see Walter Hooper's introduction to the volume *Of Other Worlds*.) Matters of ethics and personal choice which were to become so important to his adult fictions are completely nonexistent in the copious domains of Boxen. Moreover, they are noticeably lacking in the "marvellous" aspects of his later work. "My invented world was full (for me) of interest, bustle, humor, and character; but there was no poetry, even no romance, in it. It was almost astonishingly prosaic" (*SbJ*, 15). The absorbing interest of these early stories is politics. The most important character is Lord John Big of Bigham, a frog of powerful personality and Prime Minister of Boxen. We follow his career through two volumes of *Boxen: or Scenes from Boxonian City Life* and three volumes of *The Life of Lord John Big of Bigham*. The other characters are equally concerned with making a place for themselves among Boxen's rulers. Walter Hooper, Lewis's secretary, tells us that "The characters in *Scenes from Boxonian City Life* all relish a place in the 'Clique' though none of them, not even the author, appears to have any clear idea what a 'clique' is. Which is not surprising for, as Lewis wanted his characters to be 'grown-up', he naturally interested them in 'grown-up' affairs. And politics, his brother says, was a topic he almost always heard his elders discussing" (*OOW*, vii). Certainly we can detect in this singular effort an imaginative attempt to close what even at that early date before the death of his mother must have seemed an immense gap between himself and his father. Lewis recognizes quite clearly in his autobiography that Lord Big resembles his father. More than just an exercise in emulation, it was also an attempt to portray and satirize the family situation. Lord Big, for example, is described as "immense in size, resonant of voice, chivalrous (he was the hero of innumerable duels), stormy, eloquent, and impulsive" (*SbJ*, 80). Lord Big's charges, the two young kings, however, are not yet suitable replacements for their regent. They are much more concerned with their own private pleasures than with any serious political end. Throughout this piece, then, we notice Lewis's very strong ambivalence, not only toward his father but also toward himself.

These early stories also provide interest as they become material for parody for the adult writer. His later rejection of all striving for social success could not go further. Concern with politics comes to seem, especially in a figure such as Orual in the novel *Till We Have Faces*, a sign of spiritual dessication. The desire to become one of the "clique" is the basic motivation of Mark Studdock in *That Hideous Strength*, yet he finds that desire leading him into greater and greater evils.

Lewis notes, as we have seen, that his first imaginary world was "astonishingly prosaic." But his childhood was also filled with an imaginative experience of a completely different character, full of "romance" and "poetry." This experience of the romantic, which he calls in his autobiography "Joy," is perhaps the most important experience of his life. It is the touchstone by which he measures the value of every other experience. It is the basis for his love of inanimate nature and his lifelong interest in fantastic literature. Moreover, it is the basis of the wonder-filled landscapes of his adult fiction. Most simply put, it is the experience of longing or desire (Lewis uses the German word *Sehnsucht*) for that which would somehow fill up the void at the core of his family and emotional life.

When he began to read, this fundamental imaginative reflex became part of his literary experience. Everything from Beatrix Potter to Norse mythology was able to awake in him this intense desire. In fact, Lewis recounts that except for a short period during his early adolescence, this experience formed a permanent and (until his conversion) important aspect of his life.

After his disastrous experience with Oldie, Lewis attended a number of other schools. In 1910, after an unhappy term at Campbell College, he was taken ill and had to be removed from the school. Between the ages of thirteen and fifteen, he attended a small boarding school he calls Chartres. He was happy there, making friends and showing promise for the first time as a student. But there also he lost his religion. At fifteen Lewis won a scholarship to Wyvern College, a school which his brother had already attended. We have already noted the difference between Lewis's half-envying picture of the scramble in Boxen and his strongly disapproving parody of it in *That Hideous Strength*. What this shift signifies is a hardening of attitude toward his father and what his father represents. What it signifies is his retreat and ultimate disgust with the English middle class. What had been ambivalent in his attitude toward his father becomes outright hostility when confronted with the English public school.

Lewis tells us that as a result of his experience with the public school at Wyvern, he became "a Prig, a Highbrow," a member of the alienated intelligentsia spawned by, but directly opposed to, the English middle class. The change was not particularly dramatic or rapid. At first Lewis was simply a typical British schoolboy with a taste for reading. But he quickly discovered that this taste separated him from most of the rest of the school and especially from the school's social elite, a group called "the Bloods," whose only interests were sports and social life. He detested the thought of playing toady to an upperclassman. Moreover, he was very clumsy in sports. Consequently, the only routes of advancement for a lad of not very distinguished origins were closed to him. His intellectual interests were shared by only a few others. But their taste for such things, he discovered, was actually "good" taste, the best taste. Lewis later felt, however, that this consciousness of one's own intellectual superiority was already very dangerous; it "involves a kind of Fall. The moment good taste knows itself, some of its goodness is lost" (*SbJ*, 104). From that point on, the temptation to scorn the more conventional members of the school was ever present, and Lewis succumbed. To some extent this was a necessary result of the system itself. As Lewis says, it is "interesting," I think he means ironic, "that the public-school system had thus produced the very thing which it was advertised to prevent or cure. For you must understand (if you have not been dipped in that tradition yourself) that the whole thing was devised to knock the nonsense out of the smaller boys and 'put them in their place'" (*SbJ*, 104–5). Yet for Lewis, his reaction to the situation was itself a great moral evil.

Yet if Priggery was a moral disaster, it did involve an uncommon emotional clarity concerning the character of the social life at Wyvern. For Lewis the social life of the school was dominated by the struggle to achieve prominence. All other values and virtues, friendship, morality, fairness, were abandoned in the race to be popular. At Wyvern, Lewis, already something of a loner, found plenty of reasons for remaining one.

Eventually Lewis quit Wyvern and was sent to a tutor, W.T. Kirkpatrick of Bookham, to prepare for Oxford. Lewis was very happy living with Kirkpatrick and his wife. Here he was able to indulge his two passions, literature and long walks in the country. Kirkpatrick himself was very important to Lewis. From him Lewis learned the dialectical skills which were so important to his career as a Christian apologist. "If ever a man came near to being a purely logical entity, that man was Kirk. Born a little later, he would have been a logical Positivist. The idea that human beings should exercise their vocal organs for any purpose except that of communicating or discovering truth was to him preposterous. The most casual remark was taken as a summons to disputation" (*SbJ*, 135–36). It was very difficult, at first, for Lewis to defend what he calls his "vague romantic notions," but eventually he was able to contest with his master on something like an equal footing. In fact,

Lewis was so impressed by Kirkpatrick that he afterwards adopted his style of discourse for his own. John Lawlor, a student of Lewis's during the 1930s, remarks this fact, and adds that it left Lewis in the lamentable condition of being unable to engage in more mundane forms of conversation. "I could as readily as anyone deplore the influence of 'the Great Knock' [Kirkpatrick]: his meeting with Lewis was perhaps one of the least fortunate in intellectual history. The shy boy from Belfast, making his naive comments on the Surrey countryside, became the one who had no small talk; who talked habitually, as Johnson did, for victory."[14]

Lewis remarks in his autobiography that all the while he was getting on in these various schools and meeting new friends, he kept having recurring experiences of "joy." But so different was the everyday life of schoolwork and boyish comaraderie from this other experience, that it seemed to him that he was living two lives. "The two lives do not seem to influence each other at all. Where there are hungry wastes, starving for Joy, in the one, the other may be full of cheerful bustle and success; or again, where the outer life is miserable, the other may be brimming over with ecstasy" (*SbJ,* 78). What's important about this is that already in his adolescence the life of "joy," of ecstatic experience, came to seem radically distinct from the everyday life. This kind of dualism finds its way again and again into his fantasy as he creates new worlds which pose a radical alternative, an escape from mundane existence.

After one semester at Oxford in 1917, Lewis was drafted. As we have already noted, the important thing about the war for Lewis was not its harsh realities but the friends he made and the books he read. Of one occasion when he came down with "trench fever" and had to be taken to the hospital, he says, "Perhaps I ought to have mentioned before that I had had a weak chest ever since childhood and had very early learned to make a minor illness one of the pleasures of life, even in peacetime. Now, as an alternative to the trenches, a bed and a book were 'very heaven'" (*SbJ,* 189). During this time he first read Chesterton, and as he says, "I did not know what I was letting myself in for" (*SbJ,* 191). Already his atheism was beginning to crumble. This process was accelerated by the influence of another soldier, an Oxford scholar like himself, named Johnson, who was a skilled dialectician, full of "youth and whim and poetry" but above all "a man of conscience." Lewis was very attracted to his unselfconscious display of moral goodness. Lewis's own judgment about the experiences in the war is that they led him for the first time consciously on the road to theism and Christianity. But if he was learning to sing a different tune, it was played in the key of his childhood. The pattern which developed in those early years, of finding a private and personal alternative in the face of a threatening reality, is repeated again here. The reference to his childhood in his description of his wartime illness points up this connection very nicely.

After the war he returned to Oxford, and after three years there took the examination in "Greats." Although taking a "First" in the exam, he was unable to find a position teaching and decided to stay a fourth year at Oxford to study English literature. He was able to do this, however, only because of the generous financial aid of his father, who was determined that his son should find a position teaching. By then, it had become clear to both father and son that Lewis was unsuited for any profession but the academy. As Kirkpatrick had told his father, "You may make a writer or a scholar of him, but you'll not make anything else. You may make up your mind to *that*" (*SbJ*, 183). In 1925 he was elected Fellow of Magdalen College, where he remained until taking a chair at Cambridge in 1956.

In his autobiography, Lewis recounts that the path which led him back to Christianity was mainly intellectual. During these early years at Oxford, his practice of the logical virtues implanted by Kirkpatrick, strengthened by his contact with such individuals as Johnson and Owen Barfield, led him from the atheism and "popular realism" he had learned at Bookham to philosophical idealism to theism, and finally to Christianity (*SbJ*, 205). Yet more than just pure reason was involved. The crucial fact which led him to reject "popular realism" was that it caused him to doubt his experience of "joy." The new psychology had taught him that it was merely a subjective phenomenon, valuable perhaps, but certainly not real. After rejecting realism, Lewis embraced first idealism, then theism, and finally Christianity. With idealism, theism, and Christianity, he could believe that *Sehnsucht* was putting him in touch with the really real. We must not, of course, minimize the differences between these last three stages; we should especially note that Lewis was moving toward something more solid, more "normal," less "highbrow" by which to identify himself. But the fact remains that for Lewis, the authenticity of this fundamental experience could only be guaranteed by referring it to some reality outside of himself (*SbJ*, 217-21).

During this time he published his first two volumes, both of which are marked by his long interest in "romantic" literature and which clarify to some extent the issues which led him back to Christianity. The first book, a volume of poetry with the Neo-Platonic title *Spirits in Bondage,* was published in 1919. Already his conception of literature as escape was apparent in this work. The poems abound in what he called 'thoughtful wishing' (not wishful thinking), and his purpose is clearly expressed in the opening lyric:

> In my coracle of verses I will sing of lands unknown,
> Flying from the scarlet city where a Lord that knows no pity
> Mocks the broken people praying round his iron throne,
> —Sing about the Hidden Country fresh and full of quiet green,
> Sailing over seas uncharted to a port that none has seen. (*Poems,* v)

Already in this early lyric we find a distinct anticipation not only of the hidden green country of Narnia but also of the plot of one of the Narnia stories, *The Voyage of the Dawn Treader.*

In 1926, as a Fellow of Magdalen College, Lewis published *Dymer,* a long narrative poem in rime royal. It tells of a hero born in "The Perfect City":

> There you'd have thought the gods were smothered down
> Forever, and the keys were turned on fate.
> No hour was left unchartered in that town,
> And love was in a schedule and the State
> Chose for eugenic reasons who should mate
> With whom, and when. Each idle song and dance
> Was fixed by law and nothing left to chance.[15]

For a while, Dymer endures this brave new world. Finally, however, he strikes his teacher (killing him instantly), and joyfully escapes to the forest. So far this is very like the project of escape in *Spirits in Bondage.* But complications arise for Dymer which signify in Lewis a new stage of awareness about the consequences of his literary stance of revolt. Dymer's escape touches off a rebellion in which the tyrannical authorities are overthrown. But what replaces it, a continuous round of murder, arson, and pillage, is even worse. Moreover, Dymer's union with "a girl of the forest" (who is later in the poem disclosed to be a projection of his own lust) results in a monstrous offspring which wreaks great harm on men. Finally, he resolves to do battle with it and is killed. He is reborn, however, as—

> A wing'd and sworded shape, through whom the air
> Poured as through glass: and its foam-tumbled hair
> Lay white about the shoulders and the whole
> Pure body brimmed with life, as a full bowl.[16]

In this later poem we see Lewis troubled by his responsibility to society. The twin dangers of his romantic alienation from society are narcissism and anarchism, and the only way to guard the project of escape and at the same time render it morally acceptable is to anchor it in an extramundane principle of goodness. It is precisely these emotional issues which were involved in the intellectual process that led him to Christianity.

We can perhaps make this anxiety about the narcissitic tendencies of "joy" and "romanticism" more concrete by referring once more to Lewis's autobiography. Lewis recounts that he came to recognize God's claims on him slowly and with great reluctance. He insists that the greatest moral struggle he had was in overcoming the habit of privacy and introspection. Lewis's notion of a "perfect day," limned in great detail in his autobiography, is singularly solipsistic. It is a carefully orchestrated chronology of meals and work.

Recreation, such as a solitary walk after lunch, is regarded as necessary, but intercourse with others is viewed as an annoying distraction (*SbJ*, 141–43). Lewis declares that "it is a life almost entirely selfish." Lewis felt that this tendency was leading him toward the unbridled and self-centered cultivation of sensibility and subjectivity à la Symonds. His enthusiasms for "Northernness," for Norse mythology and Wagnerian music, is one of many eruptions of that "joy" which for Lewis is the most fundamental experience of his life. Yet the "joy" did not last but for a moment and his attempts to recapture it are indicative of his subjectivist tendencies. "To 'get it again' became my constant endeavor; while reading every poem, hearing every piece of music, going for every walk, I stood anxious sentinel at my own mind to watch whether the blessed moment was beginning and to endeavor to retain it if it did"(*SbJ*, 169). Lewis says that he came to realize later that he had erred in seeking the emotion itself rather than the object, or rather, the person who had caused it. "From the fading of the Northernness I ought to have drawn the conclusion that the Object, the Desirable, was further away, more external, less subjective, than even such a comparatively public and external thing as a system of mythology—had, in fact, only shone through that system" (*SbJ*, 168).

In Christianity, then, Lewis finally achieved an intellectual position which would save him from narcissim but would not jeopardize his experience of "joy." But the fact is that neither would it satisfy that experience. Christianity, especially the Anglican Christianity in which Lewis was raised, tends to be very suspicious of ecstatic emotional experiences like those of Lewis. The patient performance of one's duty is much more important than an elusive contact with some preternatural reality. In fact, from Lewis's viewpoint as a practising Christian, "joy" came to seem merely a means to an end. He says toward the end of his autobiography, "I now know that the experience, considered as a state of my own mind, had never had the kind of importance I once gave it. It was valuable only as a pointer to something other and outer"(*SbJ*, 238). Lewis states that he continued to have such experiences, but that his work as a teacher and a Christian writer were much more important to him.

Christianity, however, is a term which stands for many things. Besides a hard-nosed, aggressive critique of human nature and human society, we also find a longing for the Other World. This aspect of Christianity promises freedom from all economic and social evils, as well as that glowing realm of the impossible which so attracted Lewis. Thus, besides satisfying his need to find a place for himself in society, Christianity could also satisfy his hunger for "Otherness."

In the years after his conversion, we can see a reappearance of the split between logic and romanticism which had troubled him as a young atheist at Oxford. John Lawlor makes a very perceptive comment about Lewis's continuing interest in medieval *fyne amour* and rebellious romanticism: "Each was in some measure an opponent of, and each became in some degree a successful usurper on, the fullness of religious experience."[17]

On the one hand, we have his apologetic and philosophical writings, heavy with the influence of Kirkpatrick: *The Problem of Pain* (1940); *The Abolition of Man* (1943); *Miracles* (1947); and *Mere Christianity,* a series of talks on theology broadcast on the BBC. Included in this list should be his didactic fictions: *The Pilgrim's Regress* (1933), a barely disguised account of his own intellectual wanderings modeled on Bunyan's *Pilgrim's Progress;* his first popular success, *The Screwtape Letters* (1942), originally published weekly in the *Manchester Guardian,* and *The Great Divorce,* a short half-satiric, half-autobiographical work. We should also mention along with this aspect of his work the numerous talks on theology he gave during World War II at various R.A.F. bases. In all these works there is an amazing consistency of tone and project, a pugnacious defense of Christian orthodoxy.

As John Lawlor has said, Lewis's interest in medieval allegory and romance at times displaces Christianity at the center of his interests. Now this is undoubtedly true, but we should also realize that Lewis's scholarly interest in medieval literature and civilization feeds directly into his defense of Christianity. Beginning with *The Allegory of Love* (1936), an examination of the rise of medieval love poetry, and including his volume in the Oxford History of English Literature *English Literature in the Sixteenth Century, excluding Drama* (1944), as well as *The Discarded Image* (1964), an examination of the content and sources of the medieval world view, he has been one of this century's leading interpreters of the strengths and beauties of medieval Christian culture. It is only when he gets interested in what he calls the "mythic" qualities of medieval literature (what he might also call its "romantic" qualities) and in "worlds of fine fabling," and when he begins to say things like "the old gods had to die before they could wake again in the beauty of acknowledged myth," that Lawlor's comment makes sense.[18]

What is startling about Lewis's career as a writer is that despite his enormous success as a scholar and a Christian apologist, he continued to be intensely interested in fantastic and romantic literature. The fundamental aim of his critical writings, in such volumes as *Rehabilitations* (1939), *An Experiment in Criticism* (1961), and *Of Other Worlds* (1964), has been to establish the value of genres which come outside the realistic canons of modern literary criticism. He praises writers like George MacDonald, William Morris, H.G. Wells, David Lindsay, and E. Nesbit, and their work in such genres as the fairy romance, science fiction, and children's stories for putting readers in touch with a realm of literary experience not available to realistic fiction. As Lewis says apropos of MacDonald's myth-making abilities: "In poetry the words are the body and the 'theme' or 'content' is the soul. But in myth the imagined events are the body and something inexpressible is the soul" (*GM,* 16).

It is precisely this "something inexpressible" which Lewis at his best is able to capture. In his two science-fiction novels, *Out of the Silent Planet* and *Perelandra,* in his children's stories *The Chronicles of Narnia,* and in his re-telling of the Cupid and Psyche myth, *Till We Have Faces,* he gives his readers the magic and the mystery of great myth. Moreover, we get some of the man's amiability, a trait too often absent from his earnest but shrill apologetic and satiric writings.

Before going on to examine the fiction itself, we should mention a few of the more personal details of his later life. After his conversion Lewis still remained a loner. He entered into the life of the church community only with great reluctance. In a revealing comment, he compares going to church with going to the zoo. He much prefers, he says, to pray alone or to meet with one or two other people to discuss spiritual matters (*SbJ,* 233–34).

Though Lewis later lost some of his distaste for church-going, he never approached it with the zest he felt for masculine conversation and companionship of a group of Christian intellectual friends called the Inklings. In the introduction to *The Letters of C.S. Lewis,* his older brother, Warren Lewis, describes the character of the group's meetings and Lewis's enthusiasm for them. After tea had been drunk and pipes readied, one of the group would read a new manuscript. The group would then either praise or criticize the work. Criticism could be fierce, and Warren Lewis admitted to feeling a great deal of fear when he read the first chapter of his first book to the group. When on occasion there was nothing to read, there would just be good conversation. "On these occasions the fun would be riotous, with Jack [C.S. Lewis] at the top of his form and enjoying every minute" (*L,* 13–14).

We notice that, even to the inclusion of his brother, this circle replicates the pattern begun at home and continued at Oldie's. Only this time the threatening reality is not an individual but the secular atmosphere of society at large. In a letter of 18 February 1940, at a time when the Inklings' meetings were most frequent, Lewis writes his brother that, "The world as it is is becoming, and has partly now become, simply *too much* for people of the old square-rigged type like you and me. I don't understand its politics or its economics or any dam' thing about it."

Moreover, we should note that Lewis did not marry until he was 58. In fact, except for Mrs. Moore, the mother of an Oxford friend killed in the First World War, and his women students, whom he tended to regard with a good deal of arrogance, Lewis had very little to do with women at all. As a result his notions about women's psychology and about their place in society tended to be extremely narrow and conventional, and his fictions suffer for it. His polemics on the role of women are among the least attractive aspects of his work. During most of the years of his tenure at Oxford he lived with his brother and with Mrs. Moore, whom he called "my mother." It was not an easy life;

especially at first, money was a problem. Moreover, Mrs. Moore was always difficult to get along with. She died in 1952, and a couple of years later Lewis took Joy Davidman as his secretary. In 1956 they were married. It was a new and in many ways liberating experience for the aging don, though I find it strange that Lewis waited to marry her until she was on her death-bed, dying of cancer. Lewis, whose mother died of cancer, seems to have had a mother-complex, and any woman who got close to him was in danger of becoming his mother. But Joy experienced an almost miraculous remission and lived for another three years. As a result, Lewis gained a new and unexpected happiness. Lewis once told his close friend Nevill Coghill, "I never expected to have, in my sixties, the happiness that passed me by in my twenties" (*L*, 23). Moreover, he also gained a new depth of understanding about human love and human relations. *A Grief Observed*, written after the death of his wife, shows Lewis plunged into hitherto unknown depths of grief. As Chad Walsh observes, "When he comes up at last into the sunlight and rediscovers, in a convincing but still tentative way, the presence of God, the discovery carries more conviction to the reader than the neatly marshalled ranks of arguments in *Mere Christianity* or even the glowing Christian mythology of the interplanetary novels and Narnia tales."[19] For several years after his wife's death, Lewis was the guardian for her two teenage sons by Gresham. He died on November 22, 1963.

What, then, do we make of this writer's life? What kind of pattern do we see in it? And how do we relate it to his writings? These are the fundamental questions we have to deal with. Given the material that has just been presented, I think we can make several valid generalizations. First of all, we note that throughout his whole life there seems to run a tension between "romanticism" and "logic." Romanticism is the more important of the two and represents an imaginative response of escape to certain threatening realities, e.g., his father, his mother's death, the social life of his various schools, the war. The other sees in romanticism the dangers of narcissism and anarchy, the threat of being totally cut off from the human community. Lewis tried to reconcile these two imperatives by becoming a Christian. Christianity embodied a similar project of escape, but offered Lewis an historical and social sanction for his escape from society. Moreover, it gave him an ethical perspective from which to criticize modern society.

But these two strands were only imperfectly reconciled. Christianity has many meanings, and the dualism in Lewis's personality is reflected once again in the different meanings he gives to his Christianity. At one moment Christianity means "logic" and "philosophy," and is engaged in transforming this world. This meaning of Christianity is expressed in Lewis's polemical writings. At other moments, Christianity means "the Other World" and thereby connects with Lewis's interests in myth and fantasy. Thus Lewis reconciles the dualism but only because "Christianity" is so multivalent and ultimately contradictory in its several meanings. Thus, the dialectic reappears in the differing emphases of his work as a Christian polemicist and his work as a writer of fantasies. Moreover, the dialectic is carried on within the fantasies themselves. No one would ever mistake Lewis's books for the work of anything but a Christian writer. But the two tendencies do not fit together very well. If Lewis's basic strategy is escape, Christianity is the armor and weaponry he dons to cover his escape. But it also slows him down. Lewis's polemics keep him faced toward the enemy, modern society, he would flee. In fact, as a general rule the more explicitly Christian his writing becomes, the less it convinces the reader. But fortunately for Lewis's career as a writer, his polemical voice became less obtrusive as time went on. Gradually he came to write of worlds in which the doctrines of Christianity are often just distant parallels, adding resonance to the imagined situation. In the later work, as in all good literature, the fictional world has a strength of its own, a fullness of imagination, which will sustain the weight of Lewis's ethical concerns.

3

C.S. Lewis: The Early Fantasies

Lewis's interest in writing began, as we have seen, almost as soon as he took up pen and paper. His first efforts were directed toward the elaboration of an imaginary world called Boxen. After this first venture as a literary artist, Lewis became interested in poetry. While still an undergraduate at Oxford he published his first volume, *Spirits in Bondage*. Seven years later he published *Dymer,* a long narrative poem. In the meantime he had been elected a Fellow of Magdalen College at Oxford, and thereafter most of his time was taken up with teaching and the composition of his very readable book on medieval allegory, *The Allegory of Love*. He continued to write poetry, most of which is collected in the posthumous volume *Poems* edited by Walter Hooper, but it consists mainly of bits of polemic or of imagery which he worked out more fully in his prose. *Dymer* was his last volume of poems, although he occasionally inserted poems into a basically prose text (as in *The Pilgrim's Regress*).

Most of Lewis's writing was directed toward scholarly and polemical prose. The first fruit of his scholarly and polemical interest in the Middle Ages was *The Allegory of Love*. A tremendous success at its publication—it won the Hawthornden Prize for 1936—it continued for many years to be the standard text on medieval allegory. The book is an examination of the rise and development of what Lewis holds to be a radically new development in world literature, the poetry of courtly love. For the first time love and the relations of lovers becomes the central interest of literature, an interest which has carried over into the modern age. In this poetry, the lover is completely abased before his beloved, physically as well as emotionally. "Love sickness," in which the lover faints, swoons, and wastes away for want of his beloved, is a typical situation of this poetry. Moreover, it is a poetry of adultery; the beloved is always a married woman. Lewis suggests that both these features owe something to the fact that this poetry was written usually at court by young men whose only sure route to favor with the master was attention to the mistress. In this sense the poetry replicates the class tensions of the situation, the lover's sickness mirroring his essential lack of power in the situation as well as recognizing the danger of an aggressive sexual display toward the mistress. But more than its origins, Lewis is interested in its development from simple lyric statements to the profound psychological observation of the *Romance of the Rose* and its final accommodation with Christian morality in the work of Spenser. Thus the other main thread of Lewis's argument is to trace the development of allegory and to reveal its function as a mode of psychological realism. To Lewis's mind the best example of this function of allegory is in the *Romance of the Rose* where the psychology of love, the inner workings and conflicts of the beloved's mind, is laid out as clearly and boldly as in a nineteenth-century psychological novel. But the real high point of courtly love is when it is transformed from a poetry of adultery to a poetry of marriage. Even the *Romance of the Rose,* the most successful fusion of allegory and courtly love before Spenser, betrays the pagan character of its morality. Only in Spenser is the pagan element eliminated without sacrificing richness of presentation, and thus, Lewis maintains, the *Fairie Queene* represents the highest point in medieval literature.

It is not too early to stress that Lewis's interest in medieval lore feeds into his work both as a Christian apologist and as a fantasist. Certain images which occur in the stories constitute the tissue if not the bone of the medieval world-view. The science fiction trilogy, for example, utilizes a medieval cosmology in which everything above the moon is beneficent and well ordered and guarded by angels while the world below the moon is torn by war, threatened by tyranny, and assaulted by evil spirits. And such concepts as the cosmic dance recur again and again as Lewis reiterates the medieval view of the divine ordering of nature.

More specifically, the *Allegory of Love* presents certain ideas which suggest Lewis's views on his responsibility as a Christian writer. Perhaps the most important is the fact that he introduces extraliterary concerns (especially matters of ethics) into his literary judgments. Thus he prefers Spenser's writing to the *Romance of the Rose* not simply for its superior literary qualities (those are debatable) but for his indubitable superiority as a moralist. These extraliterary concerns become readily apparent in his discussions of certain important writers.

Lewis admires Langland, for instance, for the lofty if conventional quality of his moralism, for the sublimity of his poetic vision and for his power of rendering imaginable what before was only intelligible (i.e., Christian doctrine). Lewis strove for the same effects in his own writing. As with Langland, Lewis's "advice is as ancient, as 'conventional,' if you will, as that of Socrates; not to mention names more august." (*AL,* 158–59). Lewis sincerely believes that "It is doubtful whether any moralist of unquestioned greatness has ever attempted more (or less) than the defense of the universally acknowledged; for 'men more frequently require to be reminded than informed.'" As an observer of politics, Lewis, like Langland, "has nothing to propose except that the estates do their duty" (*AL,* 158–59).

What Lewis most admires in Spenser is what he calls "the fulness of the commonplace." He says that Spenser takes the myths and moralities of the popular imagination and deepens and enriches them with the fundamental tendencies of the generic human imagination. Spenser possesses a "mythic" sensibility. Moreover, like Langland, his morality is entirely conventional. Spenser unites the allegorical romance with the religious homilectic allegory to satirize the romance of adultery on behalf of the romance of marriage. Lewis's concern for the marriage of Mark and Jane Studdock in *That Hideous Strength* owes much to Spenser. Besides being profoundly conventional, Spenser successfully deals with matters of cosmic importance. In this regard Spenser's greatest importance for Lewis lies in his conception of nature, what one might call his Platonic naturalism. From Spenser he learned to appreciate, in George MacDonald's phrase, "The Quiet Fulness of Ordinary Nature." What this means is that, from the Christian point of view, nature is not at all ordinary. In even the smallest and most insignificant corner of nature, one can, if one looks with a Christian imagination, see the hand of God. Such a conception of nature, however, tends to be very static. For Spenser, as Lewis tells us, had learned from Plato that the good is real and evil only apparent; and from Aristotle that the natural is that which seeks the perfection of its form. Thus "Nature," the order ordained by God, is opposed to all chaos and "Mutabilitie." Yet if this is a very uncomplicated and ultimately uninteresting conception of nature, it does leave room for Lewis to express his own enthusiams for the benevolent aspects of nature. In *The Lion, the Witch, and the Wardrobe*, for instance, the once green land of Narnia has been locked in winter, imprisoned in a witch's spell for a hundred years. Suddenly, with the approach of Aslan (Christ), the spell begins to break. Spring returns, bringing hope to the witch's victims:

A strange, sweet, rustling, chattering noise—and yet not so strange, for he knew he'd heard it before—if only he could remember where! Then all at once he did remember. It was the noise of running water. All round them, though out of sight, there were streams chattering, murmuring, bubbling, splashing and even (in the distance) roaring. And his heart gave a great leap (though he hardly knew why) when he realized that the frost was over.... Only five minutes later he noticed a dozen crocuses growing round the foot of an old tree—gold and purple and white. Then came a sound even more delicious than the sound of water. Close beside the path they were following a bird suddenly chirped from the branch of a tree. (*LWW*, 115–17)

Lewis's first literary success and the book for which he is probably best known to the general audience is *The Screwtape Letters*. It was first published weekly in the Manchester *Guardian* where it eventually gained a great following. Since 1942, when it was published in book form, it has never been out of print. Typical of the admiring comments on the book of Clyde Kilby's remark that it is a "satirical classic."[1] Chad Walsh says that *The Screwtape Letters* "reveal his psychological insight and his satire at its sharpest."[2]

In general, however, this praise is overemphatic, indeed misplaced. *The Screwtape Letters* is, by far, one of the poorest showings Lewis ever made as a writer. The inspiration starts at low ebb and quickly disappears. Lewis recognized this, for in the introduction to the book, he says that writing it for the *Guardian* grew to be a terrible bore. His commitment to grinding out one of those letters every week, however, is a good indicator of his commitment to his notion of himself as a Christian writer. And the *Letters* themselves bear the marks (and the deficiencies) of that commitment.

As we have already noted in our summary of *The Allegory of Love*, Lewis considers a work of art great only when it combines lucidity and fullness of presentation with a commitment to moral and religious principles. Thus he upgrades Spenser at the expense of *Romance of the Rose* primarily on ethical grounds and despite the fact that Spenser's artistry is at times much below the level of the *Romance*. This is a permanent aspect of Lewis's thinking about aesthetics and can perhaps be made plainer by reference to his appraisal of George MacDonald. In Lewis's introduction to a selection of MacDonald's writings, he argues that MacDonald is to be valued not as a writer but as a Christian teacher. As a writer, he betrays many of the worst habits of the pulpiteer and homilist. Yet, Lewis is able to find a special kind of literary virtue in MacDonald's work, a virtue very much like that of Lewis's own work. "What he does best is fantasy—fantasy that hovers between the allegorical and the mythopoeic. And this, in my opinion, he does better than any man" (*GM*, 12–13). Nevertheless, Lewis goes on to comment that he doubts whether such mythopoetic creation is truly literary or artistic, for such a fiction does not exist in words.

Here again we see Lewis struggling with the opposition between content and form. In this particular comment, content emerges the victor as in other religious and propagandistic theories of art. And it is this kind of conception—that literatures must serve the Truth—which is reflected in the deficiencies of *The Screwtape Letters*.

It is useful to remember that *The Screwtape Letters* were written during a great burst of polemical activity during the early 1940s, including *The Personal Heresy* (1939), *The Problem of Pain* (1940), the first two series of broadcast talks (1941, 1942, and 1943), *The Abolition of Man* (1943), and *Beyond Personality* (1944).

The formula is exceedingly simple: take a Christian maxim and turn it on its head and you have advice for fledgling tempter Wormwood from His Abysmal Sublimity, his uncle, Undersecretary Screwtape. The plot, though more complicated—the twists and turns of the "patient's" moral life inscribing toward the end an ever upward curve until he is finally killed in the performance of his duty and safely out of the tempter's reach—remains more a dumb show in front of which are delivered the homilectic utterances of the Undersecretary.

To put it briefly, there is not much of artistic interest in *The Screwtape Letters.* As a piece of imaginative literature there are perhaps only two or three conceptions that should give us pause. The first of these is the metaphor of eating. Screwtape tells Wormwood, "If by steady and cool-headed application here and now you can finally secure his soul, he will then be yours forever—a brimfull living chalice of despair and horror and astonishment which you can raise to your lips as often as you please" (*SL,* 25). As Lewis says of his bad angels: "Their motive is a kind of hunger. I feign that devils can, in a spiritual sense, eat one another; and us. Even in human life we have seen the passion to dominate, almost to digest, one's fellow; to make his whole intellectual and emotional life merely an extension of one's own" (*SL,* xi). Another key conception is that of hell as a bureaucracy. "As totalitarian countries have their camps of torture, so my Hell contains deeper Hells, its 'houses of correction'" (*SL,* x). This is an extension of the kind of domination implicit in the eating metaphor. Another is the image of transformation when the enemy drops all pretense of rationality and reveals his true colors. After a particularly virulent tirade against the music and solemnity of heaven, the manuscript breaks off and is resumed in another hand which explains that in the heat of composition Screwtape had become a centipede. This is a small thing, but one that saves this particular bit of parody from going flat. I mention these elements mainly for the importance in the later, more fully developed fictional worlds of the science fiction, *Narnia,* and *Till We Have Faces.* A fourth motif, although basic thematically to the book and absolutely crucial in Lewis's later work, i.e., the quest of the individual for salvation, is not nearly so well imagined as the endless squabblings and rivalries of the devils. The patient and his world are ghost figures by comparison.

For the rest, we see Lewis attacking all that is modish or simply modern. He opposes all modernism, evolutionism, materialism, and historicism with the traditional Christian verities. Screwtape tells his nephew:

> The greatest triumph of all is to elevate this horror of the Same Old Thing into a philosophy so that nonsense in the intellect may reinforce corruption in the will. It is here that the general Evolutionary or Historical character of modern European thought comes in so usefully. The Enemy loves platitudes. Of a proposed course of action He wants men, so far as I can see, to ask very simple questions: Is it righteous? . . . . How, if we can keep men asking: "Is it in accordance with the general movement of our times?" they will neglect the relevant questions. (*SL,* 118)

Obviously the problem with this is that at many points we begin to hear Lewis's own voice. At times this kind of thing gets really out of hand and Lewis loses all control of his imaginative conception. In order to make his point loudly and clearly enough, he will turn off the Undersecretary's microphone and feed his own voice directly into the P.A. system. After the patient's successful death, Screwtape berates his nephew, telling him:

All the delights of sense or heart or intellect with which you could once have tempted him, even the delights of virtue itself, now seem to him in comparison but as the half-nauseous attractions of a raddled [sic] harlot would seem to a man who hears that his true beloved whom he has loved all his life and whom he had believed to be dead is alive and even now at his door. He is caught up into that world where pain and pleasure take on transfinite value and where all our arithmetic is dismayed. Once more, the inexplicable meets us. (SL, 148)

This is quite impossible for any wrong-minded or consistent devil. It is the rhetoric of a not very capable didactic author.

After the success of The Screwtape Letters, Lewis was assured an audience for everything he produced. His science fiction trilogy, Out of the Silent Planet (1938), Perelandra (1943), and That Hideous Strength (1945), achieved a considerable success of its own, both with readers and critics. Gilbert Highet says that he has read it a half-dozen times and that it haunts him, representing as it does worlds that are "terrifying and beautiful." Marjorie Hope Nicholson calls Out of the Silent Planet "the most beautiful of all cosmic voyages and in some ways the most moving."[3]

The trilogy, like The Screwtape Letters, was written during Lewis's great burst of polemical writing during the late 1930s and 1940s, and this polemical interest is reflected in the stories, especially in That Hideous Strength. It is this aspect of the work that The London Times picks up when it says that Lewis was writing "brilliantly imagined and exciting 'science fiction' to convey a deep conviction about God and about living with a subtlety and symbolic power perhaps to be found elsewhere only in the works of his beloved Edmund Spenser."[4] In a similar vein, Gilbert Highet says that Lewis's imaginary worlds exhibit "a mysticism that is at once poetic and religious" and R.J. Reilly that all three volumes involve an attempt "to throw over esoteric landscapes the holy light of Joy."[5] As these comments suggest, in the trilogy Lewis often was able to reconcile his religious commitment and his concerns as a fantasist and an artist. But there are still plenty of other times when Lewis's polemical intention overrides his artistic concerns.

Moreover, the tension between individualism, with its psychological and social dangers, and commitment to a social group, a theme which had been important not only in Dymer but also in The Pilgrim's Regress, provides the major narrative and thematic interest in the novels. In its own way, this theme mirrors Lewis's basic artistic problem: will he guarantee the Christianity of his writing or will he concern himself primarily with "realizing" his fictional world? Either decision presents him with a problem. If he is always letting the reader know he is reading a Christian author, he runs the risk of destroying the "reality" and power of his imaginary world. If he concentrates on achieving a rich and fully imagined presentation, he cannot guarantee that anyone will get the point. As this problem works itself out on the artistic and narrative levels, however, Lewis and his characters opt for polemic.

The story of the trilogy consists of three loosely related actions. *Out of the Silent Planet* opens at twilight in a rather deserted part of England. A Cambridge philologist named Ransom, who bears numerous similarities to Lewis, is on a walking tour. He is stopped by a local woman who asks him if he will stop at a neighboring house to ask for her boy. She explains that the boy works there and is late returning. Ransom finds the boy involved in a scuffle with two men, one whom he recognizes as an old schoolmate of his named Devine. The other is introduced as a famous physicist named Weston. The boy is sent home but Ransom, his guard down, is given knock-out drops and is kidnapped by the pair. When he wakes up, he finds he is 85,000 miles from earth heading into space. During the trip he learns about Weston's plans to colonize space. He also learns that he is being taken to a strange planet as a human sacrifice for an alien race named the Sorns. They land and set up camp. When the Sorns arrive, Ransom discovers that they are monstrously tall and white. He manages to escape and, near madness, wanders for a day and a half in the Martian wilderness. At last he encounters a large otter-like creature, which he at first thinks is dangerous, but then realizes is rational. He spends an idyllic time living with this creature and its kind, the Hrossa, and learning their language. After a time he receives a summon from the Oyarsa, the ruler of the planet, to come to his seat at Meldilorn. Ransom is reluctant and instead joins a hunt with the Hrossa for a dangerous water-beast. The beast is killed with Ransom's help but immediately upon landing, his friend Hyoi, the Hross who befriended him, is shot and killed by one of the kidnappers. Bereft and admonished, Ransom immediately sets off for Meldilorn. On the way he encounters a Sorn who helps him and teaches him more of Malacandra (Mars) and its peoples. At Meldilorn he surveys the historical tablets, which closely parallel certain myths and legends on earth, and learns their meaning from the Oyarsa. He hears that the stories in the Bible are true. He is told of a fallen eldil (angel) who revolted against Maleldil (God) and who now wants to destroy Maleldil's creation. Up until recently the Bent One had been confined to earth, but with the help of Weston and Devine he plans to bring his evil to the rest of the universe. Weston arrives at Meldilorn with his prophecy of destruction for all nonhuman races and is chastised. The Oyarsa gives Ransom the admonition to "Watch those two bent ones. Be courageous. Fight them." Finally he sends Ransom and the other two back to earth.

Ransom's chance to "fight them" comes soon enough in *Perelandra* when he is summoned to Venus (Perelandra) by the Oyarsa. He arrives there in a coffin and finds a beautiful green woman who is to be the mother of a new race. The story of the garden of paradise is to be repeated here, for the tempter soon appears in the person of Weston. He plummets from the sky in his spacecraft. But it is not the same Weston whom Ransom had known. Rather it is the body of Weston powered by a devil. The temptation begins as a debate, with Ransom entering the debate against the tempter. The green Lady does not succumb, but the temptation goes on. And on. And on, with Ransom losing, the devil gaining, and the Lady in danger. Finally, Ransom realizes that if he is going to save the Lady, he will have to use something stronger than words. When the Oyarsa had said "fight," he had meant literally just that. Although convinced that he will be killed, he resolves to fight the demon. After an epic battle, Ransom kills the tempter. He recovers, meets the Lady, now rejoined to her King, watches as the Oyarsa of Perelandra turns over the governance of the planet to the two "humans" and enjoys the ensuing vision of the cosmic dance. He returns to earth marvelously transformed, a forty-year-old man who looks twenty, in perfect health except where the fiend had bitten him on the foot.

In *That Hideous Strength* Ransom remains in the background during the first part of the book. The book opens with the faltering marriage of Mark and Jane Studdock. Jane is a former scholar who feels trapped as a housewife. Mark is an ambitious young sociologist who doesn't pay enough attention to his wife. She is suffering from a series of horrible and vivid nightmares. On the advice of a friend named "Mother" Dimble, she finally goes to an old woman with the daunting name of Grace Ironwood who owns an estate named St. Anne's. There Jane meets a friendly young woman named Camilla Denniston and learns from Miss Ironwood that her dreams have nothing to do with her psychological state, but rather are information about an imminent attack by the forces of evil on the human race. Meanwhile, her husband Mark is getting deeply involved with the National Institute for Coordinating Experiments (NICE), whose mottos "Cut Out Red Tape" and "Rehabilitation, Not Punishment" mask a completely brutal disregard for traditional human rights. The demons, who are prompting the leaders of the NICE, hope to create as much pain and suffering as they can, but more especially to win as many souls as possible. After a narrow escape from the NICE police, Jane goes to live at St. Anne's with Miss Ironwood, Ransom, the Dennistons, the now-dispossessed Dimbles, her former servant Mrs. Maggs, as well as a bear named Mr. Bultitude, and a raven named Baron Corvo. Mark, although his life is threatened, eventually refuses to cooperate with the NICE. Finally, a resurrected Merlin and the assembled powers of heaven destroy the NICE and all its works. The marriage is restored and the threat to the human race is ended.

Given the decidedly didactic bent of *The Screwtape Letters* and the knowledge that the trilogy incorporates such mighty Christian archetypes as the temptation in Paradise, the revolt of the angels, Babel, as well as a cosmology straight out of the sixteenth century, we might expect a rather bald-faced allegory, continually imposing itself on the integrity of the characters and distracting our interest from the story. This does happen, of course, but we would be very much mistaken to suppose it to be the general effect. For the trilogy as an imaginative creation stands far above *The Screwtape Letters*.

Lewis is more careful that his characters exist in their own right and not simply on behalf of some overriding religious or moral abstraction. His statement in an introductory note to *Perelandra*, "All the human characters in this book are purely fictitious and none of them is allegorical," indicates an awareness of the problem, especially with characters like the Green Lady. Allegory, Lewis maintains in *The Allegory of Love*, generates a univocal meaning. But Lewis himself is delighted by the equivocal. Lewis says that his fictions exist at a point in time where the marvelous known-to-be-fiction has replaced the marvelous known-to-be-fact. Only when mythology declined from a system of belief to a species of ornamentation, i.e., when it ceased to be an object of love or hate, was it thereby freed to suggest an eternity and a remoteness and a peace for its own sake (*AL*, 65, 75, 82). So with the cosmology and angelolgy of the Middle Ages. Consider this speculation during Ransom's journey to Mars:

> He wondered how he could ever have thought of planets, even of the earth, as islands of life and reality floating in a deadly void. Now, with a certainty which never after deserted him, he saw the planets—the "earths" he called them in his thought—as mere holes or gaps in the living heaven—excluded and rejected wastes of heavy matter and murky air, formed not by addition to, but by subtraction from, the surrounding brightness. And yet, he thought, beyond the solar system, the brightness ends. Is that the real voice, the real death? Unless... he groped for the idea... unless visible light is also a hole or gap, a mere diminution of something else. Something that is to bright unchanging heaven as heaven is to the dark, heavy earths.... (*OSP*, 40)

Obviously he is pointing us toward the Christian God, but not as the familiar and comfortable spirit who presides over brick churches and Sunday observance, but rather as the mysterious, unfathomable, omnipotent, and yet strangely beneficent ruler of the infinite heavens. The stories do not simply act out, then, the familiar doctrines of Christian theology. Instead the doctrine, as myth and archetype, exists for the story, giving deeper suggestiveness and solemnity to the landscapes and the actions of the characters.

We see this conception most clearly in Lewis's discussion of science fiction, especially in the essays contained in the posthumous volume, *Of Other Worlds*. In "Of Science Fiction," for example, he categorizes the various "sub-species" of science fiction. Lewis sees, in such works as *1984* or Wells's *When the Sleeper Wakes*, that the leap into the future can be used as a viewpoint for criticizing and satirizing tendencies present in contemporary society. Lewis's intent in *That Hideous Strength* (set "after the war") is obviously polemical and satiric. Typically science fiction is speculative and involves the examination of human reactions in a vastly different setting. Here again Wells is Lewis's model, this time in *First Men on the Moon*. Lewis uses this approach with telling moral force in *Out of the Silent Planet* when Ransom, bringing expectations shaped by a fallen, war-torn world and by a secularized, humanistic world-view to an unfallen world, displays a paralyzing and unreasonable fear of everything and everyone. Even more speculative are eschatological works which picture the ultimate destiny of the race. *The Time Machine* and *Childhood's End* are two well-known examples of such work, and Lewis's own novels abound with such speculations. In the trilogy we are told that Mars must die, that Earth will die, that even Venus will die, but that the cosmic dance will go on. These concerns even invade the children's stories, as in the apocalyptic conclusion of the Narnia stories, *The Last Battle.*

But the one "sub-species" Lewis is most interested in involves what he calls "an imaginative impulse as old as man." Works from Homer to Grimm, to George MacDonald, David Lindsay, Tolkien, and Mervyn Peake create worlds not tied to probability, worlds whose primary function is the evocation of wonder and beauty.

> The marvellous is in the grain of the whole work. We are, throughout, in another world. What makes that world valuable is not, of course, mere multiplication of the marvellous either for comic effect or for mere astonishment, but its quality, its flavor. If good novels are comments on life, good stories of this sort (which are very much rarer) are actual additions to life; they give, like certain rare dreams, sensations we never had before, and enlarge our conception of the range of possible experience. (*OOW*, 70)

What these stories *mean* or what they point to is a question Lewis finds himself unable to answer. "I am not sure that anyone has satisfactorily explained the keen, lasting, and solemn pleasure which such stories can give. Jung, who went furthest, seems to me to produce as his explanation one more myth which affects us in the same way as the rest. Surely the analysis of water should not itself be wet?" (*OOW*, 71). What seems to be much more important about these stories is what they *do*, and what they do, as he points out in this essay and in other works (such as *An Experiment in Criticism*, where the point applies to literature in general) is to allow the reader an imaginative escape not only from concrete actuality but also from the limitations involved in being a finite individual.

In a similar vein, Lewis criticized as "bad reading...the belief that all good books are good primarily because they give us knowledge, teach us 'truths' about 'life'" (*EC*, 74). This comment is a far cry from the positions Lewis took in *The Allegory of Love* and in the introduction to *George MacDonald: An Anthology* where he sought to connect a writer's greatness with his commitment to Christian truth. We see Lewis making an important reorientation in his aesthetics. It was a change that had beneficial results for his writing, results which first made their appearance in the science-fiction trilogy.

This radical improvement between *The Screwtape Letters* and the trilogy may be also traced to a change in Lewis's compositional technique. Lewis started from an imagined picture, devoid of narrative meaning but fraught with portent. For instance, "The starting point of the second novel, *Perelandra,* was my mental picture of the floating islands. The whole of the rest of my labours in a sense consisted of building up a world in which floating islands could exist. And then, of course, the story about an averted fall developed. This is because as you know, having your people go to this exciting country, something must happen" (*OOW,* 74). There is something a lot more spontaneous and genuine in this kind of composition than in the made-to-order composition of *The Screwtape Letters.* By starting from these genuinely imaginative materials he was able to forge the union of mythic and fictive materials which makes the trilogy at times so beautiful. A particularly fine example is the conception and description of the Martian landscape.

> He tried hard to make out something of the farther shore. A mass of something purple, so huge that he took it for a heather-covered mountain, was his first impression: on the other side, beyond the larger water, there was something of the same kind. But there, he could see over the top of it. Beyond were strange upright shapes of whitish green: too jagged and irregular for buildings, too thin and steep for mountains. Beyond and above these again was the rose-coloured cloud-like mass. It might really be a cloud, but it was very solid-looking and did not seem to have moved since he first set eyes on it. It looked like the top of a gigantic red cauliflower—or like a huge bowl of red soapsuds—and it was exquisitely beautiful in tint and shape. (*OSP,* 43)

This is a "gothic" world, in which everything seems to be reaching as far as it can for something that will free it, in Lewis's words, "of the limitations of self." When he realizes that the strange shapes of whitish green are mountains, he understands that "here was the full statement of the *perpendicular* theme which beast and plant and earth all played on Malacandra—here in this riot of rock, leaping and surging skyward like solid jets from some rock-fountain, and hanging by their own lightness in the air, so shaped, so elongated, that all terrestrial mountains must ever after seem to him to be mountains lying on their sides. He felt a life and lightening at the heart" (*OSP,* 53). What is especially appealing about these descriptions is the way Lewis takes a physical fact—the difference between gravity on earth and on Mars—and makes it the basis for imagery full of wonder and of what he calls in *An Experiment in Criticism* "the numinous." "The recurrent efforts of the mind to grasp—we mean chiefly, to conceptualize—this something, are seen in the persistent tendency to provide myths with allegorical explanations. And after all allegories have been tried, the myth itself continued to feel more important than they" (*EC,* 44). Like the transformation of space into heaven—although that is not so well grounded in physical fact—this landscape "enlarges our conception of the range of possible experience." The book is filled with similar beauties, beauties which separate it from more ordinary forms of science fiction.

But they are also very different from Lewis's own more didactic materials (even the ones in *Out of the Silent Planet*). Fictions like a language (which we never hear) shared by all the planets in the solar system, supposed communication between planets in prehistoric times, the hidden unity of Martian and earthly mythologies, all embody a polemical thrust. All are intended to create a sense of objectivity and distance from earthly culture. This becomes most dramatically effective in the scene where Ransom translates Weston's metabiological schemes and romantic posturings into what appear to be the simpler and more direct terms of the solar language. For example, Weston tells the Oyarsa, "To you I may seem a vulgar robber, but I bear on my shoulders the destiny of the human race." Ransom, tediously and deflatingly translates this as, "Among us, Oyarsa, there is a kind of *hnau* [rational being] who will take other *hnaus'* food and—and things, when they are not looking. He says he is not an ordinary one of that kind. He says what he does now will make very different things happen to those of our people who are not yet born." Similarly, when Weston, in a characteristically inflated vein, insists that "our right to supersede you is the right of the higher over the lower," Ransom translates this as "he says it would not be the act of a bent *hnau* if our people killed all your people" (*OSP*, 135–36).

One can appreciate the point Lewis is making while realizing that it is just a little too pat. This is no more than the typical dyslogistic translation common to all polemical writings. You make your opponent say much worse things than he actually says. *The Screwtape Letters* is founded on just such a principle. This whole range of images is as abstract as anything in *Screwtape*. The Oyarsa, the angelic spirit who guides the destiny of Mars, often reveals himself as the angelic counterpart of Screwtape. He tells Ransom how the Bent One revolted against Maleldil, that there was a great war, and that Maleldil did great things wrestling with the Bent One on Thulcandra (Earth, the silent planet).

The contrast between genuinely imaginative writing and a more abstract polemical style is a basic stylistic feature of the trilogy. In the one, the pleasure of the literary experience is enough to bring the reader into Lewis's imagined world. In the other, we are taken out of the imagined world and into the world of Christian discourse (which cannot be merely pleasurable but must also be authoritative). At such times the benign and attractive world of Malacandra, with its strange peoples, its lush purples, greens, and reds, is used as a mere pretext for the preaching of Christian dogma.

Yet in the end it is the polemic which dominates. The Oyarsa and his speeches completely dominate the last section of the book. Moreover, this pattern is repeated in *Perelandra*. At first we are given another strange and wondrous landscape, vastly different from that of Mars but equally appealing.

His first impression was of nothing more definite than of something slanted—as though he were looking at a photograph which had been taken when the camera was not held level. And even this lasted only for an instant. The slants rushed together and made a peak, and the peak flattened suddenly into a horizontal line, and the horizontal line tilted and became the edge of a vast gleaming slope which rushed furiously towards him. At the same moment he felt that he was being lifted. Up and up he soared till it seemed as if he must reach the burning dome of gold that hung above him instead of a sky. Then he was at a summit; but almost before his glance had taken in a huge valley that yawned beneath him—shining green like glass and marbled with streaks of scummy white—he was rushing down into that valley at perhaps thirty miles an hour. And now he realised that there was a delicious coolness over every part of him except his head, that his feet rested on nothing, and that he had for some time been performing unconsciously the actions of a swimmer. He was riding the foamless swell of an ocean, fresh and cool after the fierce temperatures of Heaven, but warm by earthly standards—as warm as a shallow bay with sandy bottom in a sub-tropical climate. As he rushed smoothly up the great convex hillside of the next wave he got a mouthful of the water. It was hardly at all flavoured with salt; it was drinkable; it was drinkable—like fresh water and only, by an infinitesimal degree, less insipid. Though he had not been aware of thirst till now, his drink gave him a quite astonishing pleasure. It was almost like meeting Pleasure itself for the first time. He buried his flushed face in the green translucence, and when he withdrew it, found himself once more on the top of a wave. (*P*, 34–35)

On first encounter this passage is very dissociating and very exciting. It is also (except for one sentence toward the end) completely concrete. But this kind of interest is quickly put aside in favor of a re-enactment of the Temptation of Eve (only this time with a happy ending), in which numerous and lengthy speeches on the place of a wife, on the danger of pride, and other matters important to a Christian apologist but not to the ordinary reader take over.

That Hideous Strength, the last novel in the trilogy, is, by common consensus, the weakest of the three. It involves a complete reversion to the Christian didacticism of *The Screwtape Letters.* Ransom, now king of Logres, the "real" spiritual Britain, says such tremendously pompous things as, "Courtship knows nothing of equality; nor does fruition. No one has ever told you that obedience—humility—is an erotic necessity." There is no fantasy at all in this novel or if there is it is very sadistic, a kind of polemical fantasy, as when Merlin obliterates the NICE.

Thus Lewis is ultimately more committed to a notion of fiction that is overtly polemical. Yet the stylistic contrast which we notice especially in the first two novels suggest a vital ethical problem or tension which becomes in the person of Ransom and later in Jane and Mark thematically important. The problem is essentially the same as in *Dymer* where self-assertion leads to anarchy and solipsism. Ransom is accused of solipsism; Mark and Jane of selfishness. Ransom totters on the brink of madness. The Studdock's marriage and the fate of humanity rest on Jane's surrender of her "selfish" desire to be her own woman.

This reflects the tension we have already examined in Lewis's own life between the need to escape from a threatening world into a private world of fantasy and the anxiety he felt over such a solipsistic retreat, as well as the positive need for contact with a human community. It is precisely these latter concerns which led him to Christianity, thereby guaranteeing with its "truth" the project of escape which formed a basic aspect of Lewis's personality. The trilogy is begun nearly ten years after Lewis's conversion, yet it embodies nearly the same ethical concerns that went into *Dymer*, written in 1925. What this suggests is that even after his conversion Lewis continued to be intensely interested in private fantasy worlds and to be harassed by the solipsistic aspects of such activity.

From this thematic viewpoint, the science fiction trilogy may be seen as a three stage process of spiritual development in which (1) the soul receives its call to God, (2) the soul overcomes it own worst self, and (3) the soul sets out to do God's work in the world. It is not for nothing that the hero is called Ransom or that when we first meet him, he is "the Pedestrian"(shades of John Bunyan).

The first of these stages involves the creation of an anti-science-fiction novel, that is, it involves the main character in a process of overcoming a set of pernicious expectations inculcated by earlier science fiction stories. As has already been pointed out, this does not mean that Lewis disapproves of science fiction generally or even of H.G. Wells, whom he cites as being most responsible for what he considers an insidious conception of alien beings. What we get in Wells's stories, *The War of The Worlds* and *The Time Machine*, is monsters and a pitched battle between *them* and *us*. In an interview given in 1963, Lewis views the growing humility of recent science fiction as a good thing. "Most of the earlier stories start from the assumption that we, the human race, are in the right, and everything else is ogres; I may have done a little towards altering that, but the new point of view has come very much in. We've lost our confidence, so to speak. This is surely an enormous gain—a humane gain" (*OOW*, 77).

In *Out of the Silent Planet*, then, Ransom is busy unlearning the stock responses of a scientific, secularistic, and humanistic age. We have seen his surprise at the glories of the heavens. Moreover, when he gets to Mars, he escapes his human kidnappers and finds a nonhuman rational being. At first he is afraid and thinks it merely a big, dangerous animal. But soon he discovers that it is friendly and really quite intelligent. Yet despite these experiences and the fact that he is a Christian, he is still unwilling to go to the Oyarsa, the strange being "who neither breathes nor dies." Only after repeated admonitions and the tragic death of his alien friend, Hyoi, does he finally obey the summons of Oyarsa. And the result is a tremendous surprise, for the being he meets is neither more nor less than an angel directly descended of medieval imaging, one of the spirits who guided the planets on their cosmic journeys. There is no talk here about centrifugal or centripetal forces. Ransom learns that the universe is a lot more friendly than he expected. He only has to approach it in the proper way.

Yet before he achieves this vision of peace and serenity, he experiences moments of dissociation close to madness. For instance, after Ransom escapes from his kidnappers, he wanders by himself for quite a long while. The shock of his adventure and the strange surrounding tax his physical and emotional capacities almost to the breaking point.

> Then he remembered with inexpressible relief that there was a man wandering in the wood—poor devil—he'd be glad to see him. He would come up to him and say, "Hullo, Ransom,"—he stopped, puzzled. No, it was only himself: it *was* Ransom. Or was he? Who was the man whom he had led to a hot Stream and tucked up in bed, telling him not to drink the strange water? (*OSP*, 51)

This psychological splitting (a kind of fiction, not unlike the creation of imaginary worlds) results from Ransom's complete isolation from the human community. But this isolation is only an aggravation of the situation which Ransom himself desires. Lewis wants us to feel that Ransom is much too self-involved. We find him at the beginning of the book taking a walking tour (one of Lewis's favorite pastimes) and revelling in his freedom. "On a walking tour," he tells Devine, "you are absolutely detached. You stop where you like and go on when you like. As long as it lasts you need consider no one and consult no one but yourself" (*OSP*, 16). And Devine, taking the hint, realizes that such a person, with no attachments anywhere, would be a perfect victim for a kidnapping.

Acting as ideological blinders, which force him back on himself and thus threaten madness, are Ransom's expectations about the creatures he will find on Mars. "His mind, like so many minds of his generation, was richly furnished with bogies. He had read his H.G. Wells and others. His universe was peopled with horrors such as ancient and medieval mythology could hardly rival. No insect-like, vermiculate or crustacean Abominable, no twitching feelers, rasping wings, slimy coils, curling tentacles, no monstrous union of superhuman intelligence and insatiable cruelty seemed to him anything but likely on an alien world" (*OSP*, 35). Hence his flight and his reluctance to face Oyarsa. Modern man, even a religious man, is afraid that the only spirits he'll find are going to be evil spirits.

Yet given the fact that Ransom was raised and educated on a planet torn by war and class strife, it is no surprise that he would flee the Martians. In fact, the flight, though dangerous to Ransom himself, is a polemical thrust, like its counterpart in *Dymer*.

These pernicious social relations are embodied and criticized in the figures of Devine and Weston. Unlike Ransom, they are both successful and important, yet they represent the Demonic Principle, Modern Department, Scientific Branch, as first adumbrated in *Screwtape* and polemically attacked in such works as *The Abolition of Man.* For Lewis, Devine is the perfect product of modern education; he believes in nothing save his own whim or self-interest. As Screwtape had said, "Your man has been accustomed, ever since he was a boy, to having a dozen incompatible philosophies dancing about together inside his head. He doesn't think of doctrines as primarily 'true' or 'false,' but as 'academic' or 'practical,' 'outworn' or 'temporary,' 'conventional' or 'ruthless.' Jargon, not argument, is your best ally in keeping him from the church" (*SL*, 8). And Devine is certainly one of those for whom intellectual and religious questions are merely matters for impious wit. "Devine had learned just half a term earlier than anyone else that kind of humor which consists in a perpetual parody of the sentimental or idealistic cliches of one's elders" (*OSP*, 15). Worse even than his impiety, however, is the pall cast by analysis over his emotions. He can't enjoy anything spontaneously, the way Ransom enjoys a walk or a book. Everything is judged according to whether it benefits his own self-interest or not. He can't conceive that "the good of it" would be reason enough. But worst of all is his callous disregard for the rights of others in his own climb to the top. He would willingly have Ransom or the boy die, if it would increase his wealth or power. In the figure of Devine, Lewis is expressing some of his own disgust at the social life of his public school. Devine and Ransom, the Lewis-surrogate in the novel, had, after all, once been schoolmates.

Devine is the type of simple selfishness. Weston is a more complicated case. He shows signs of selfishness, excessive ambition, and a lust for power. Devine introduces him as "*the* Weston, the great physicist. Has Einstein on toast and drinks a pint of Shrodinger's blood for breakfast" (*OSP*, 15). A grisly image, as appropriate to Devine as to Weston, it reminds us of the eating metaphor in *The Screwtape Letters.* But this is Devine's bantering, cynical way of putting things. Weston, on the other hand, sees himself as completely unselfish, as having dedicated himself entirely to the future betterment of the race. Weston, however, is a misguided idealist whose activities point up the danger of reforming and modernizing the traditional system of values. For example, while debating whether to take the idiot boy Harry or the don Ransom as a human sacrifice to Mars, Devine and Weston have the following exchange:

> "The boy was ideal," said Weston sulkily. "Incapable of serving humanity and only too likely to propagate idiocy. He was the sort of boy who in a civilized community would be automatically handed over to a state laboratory for experimental purposes."
>
> "I dare say. But in England he is the sort of boy in whom Scotland Yard might conceivably feel an interest. This busybody, on the other hand, will not be missed for months...."
>
> "Well, I confess I don't like it. He is, after all, human. The boy was really almost a—a preparation. Still, he's only an individual, and probably a quite useless one. We're risking our own lives too. In a great cause...."(*OSP, 19*)

"Almost a—a preparation." For Lewis, the hesitation is crucial. He wants to show us that Weston's morality doesn't come from the heart, but is fabricated as a rationalization for his own lust for success and power. He is constantly improvising, to suit the expediency of the moment. The test of any morality, for Lewis, is how well you treat individual human beings. Do your actions measure up to the laws of beneficence and justice, to the duties to children and the aged? Obviously Weston's actions fail this test miserably; they fail even to take individuals into any account.

If Lewis were to give a coherent account of Weston's philosophy, it would be something like this. In a secularized world, one without God and consequently without immortality, there is no transcendence and no meaning for the individual human life. The only transcendence is that achieved by the intellectual and material progress of the race. The most the individual can do is to become part of that drive for progress and expedite the development of the race. Anything that hinders that onward rush must be eliminated. "You cannot be so small-minded," he tells Ransom, "as to think that the rights or the life of an individual or of a million individuals are of the slightest importance in comparison with this" (*OSP*, 27). But his thought is further complicated by the fact that Weston has ever before him the image (painted best by Wells in *The Time Machine*) of the final extinction of life on the planet Earth. His plan is to colonize other planets and extirpate the natives and to keep on planet-hopping as one sun after another dies. Ultimately this racist philosophy involves him in the utmost barbarism and savagery. Quite clearly it is an offshoot of Herbert Spencer's social Darwinism, and Lewis's answer is quite simple and clear: you may be stronger, but that doesn't mean you're better (morally, emotionally, or even intellectually). Obviously Ransom has very good reasons for wanting to shun this kind of person, even if it means being totally alone.

This primary reaction is symbolized in an important passage at the beginning of the book. The dream which Ransom has after being drugged by Devine is a striking example of Lewis's capacity for compressed statement:

> It seemed to him that he and Weston and Devine were all standing in a little garden surrounded by a wall. The garden was bright and sunlit, but over the top of the wall you could see nothing but darkness. They were trying to climb over the wall and Weston asked them to give him a hoist up. Ransom kept on telling him not to go over the wall because it was so dark on the other side, but Weston insisted, and all three of them set about doing so. Ransom was the last. He got astride on the top of the wall, sitting on his coat because of the broken bottles. The other two had already dropped down on the outside into darkness, but before he followed them a door in the wall—which none of them had noticed—was opened from without and the queerest people he had ever seen came into the garden bringing Weston and Devine back with them. They left them in the garden and retired into the darkness themselves, locking the door behind them. Ransom found it impossible to get down from the wall. He remained sitting there, not frightened but rather uncomfortable because his right leg, which was on the outside, felt so dark and his left leg felt so light. "My leg will drop off if it gets much darker," he said. Then he looked down into the darkness and asked "Who are you?" and the Queer People must still have been there for they all replied, "Hoo—Hoo—Hoo?" just like owls. (*OSP*, 18).

Obviously the main thrust of this passage is polemical, its primary intention to discredit Weston and Devine in the eyes of the reader. The light and dark imagery is just a little too obvious in sorting out the good and the bad. Yet still in all, this passage has a resonance about it that makes it stick in the mind. It has something to do with the split we see revealed in Ransom and also with the curiously detached delivery of the statement, "My leg will drop off if it gets much darker." But it has even more to do with the fact that the garden is small and limited and surrounded by the darkness. What's working here, in this contrast between inside and outside, are the ambiguities about subjectivity which haunt Lewis. Perhaps we can see in the garden an autobiographical reference to the childhood situation in which the house and its grounds, the workroom, and the privacy of one's own imagination were seen as refuges from some exterior threat. The garden, after all, is certainly man-made, and as an artifact of the human will it relates to the activity of a writer. Yet if the inside is attractive to Ransom, in contrast to the exterior darkness, it is ambiguous of itself. For it is a prison kept by some very sinister guards. Ransom achieves a stable outlook on the universe, one which frees him of the terrors of madness, only when he realizes that the darkness is on the inside (on the planets) and the light is on the outside (in the heavens).

But this image of the subjectivity imprisoned in itself retains a qualified approval. It is not until *Perelandra,* when Ransom overcomes his own worst self, that the full horrors of subjectivity are revealed. As can be seen at the beginning of the novel, he has still to heal the dangerous split in his nature, which we first saw pictured in his straddling the fence. He wears the image of it on his very skin. "He glanced down at himself. Certainly his legs presented an odd spectacle, for one was brownish-red (like the flanks of a Titian satyr) and the other was white—by comparison almost a leprous white" (*P,* 55). As a matter of fact, he is once again all too ready to set out on his own. "As soon as the Lady was out of sight Ransom's first impulse was to run his hands through his hair, to expel breath from his lungs in a long whistle, to light a cigarette, to put his hands in his pockets, and in general, to go through all that ritual of relaxation which a man performs on finding himself alone after a rather trying interview" (*P,* 72). But since he has accepted the Oyarsa's call, he must do something to prove the completeness of his commitment.

His test involves the moral struggle to decide whether he will physically battle the demon. But Ransom's real battle is with himself and the horrible fantasies which he imagines. "Vivid pictures crowded upon him. . . . the deadly cold of those hands. . . . the long metallic nails. . . . ripping off narrow strips of flesh, pulling out tendons. One would die slowly"(*P,* 143). Thus Ransom's real enemy is once again his own diseased subjectivity.

Yet the battle is almost as bad as he had imagined. He wins, but only after tremendous physical suffering. It is as if Ransom were living out his worst subjective fantasy in order that he might be inoculated against it forever. But this fear is connected with a more general modern anxiety about the meaninglessness of life in general. This anxiety is the product of modern scientific concepts like indeterminacy and relativity. Even Ransom is not immune to the impact of this "Empirical Bogey," "the great myth of our century with its gases and galaxies, its light years and evolutions, its nightmare perspectives of simple arithmetic in which everything that can possibly hold significance for the mind becomes the mere by-product of essential disorder" (*P*, 164). But Weston represents the end-product of this view of things. During his battle with Ransom, his nerve breaks and he tells what it is really like to be a damned soul:

> Picture the universe as an infinite globe with this very thin crust on the outside. But remember its thickness is the thickness of *time*. It's about seventy years thick in the best places. We are born on the surface of it and all our lives we are sinking through it. When we've got all the way through then we are what's called Dead: we've got into the dark part inside, the real globe. If your God exists, He's not in the globe—He's outside, like a moon. As we pass into the interior we pass out of His ken. He doesn't follow us in. You would express it by saying He's not in time—which you think comforting! In other words He stays put: out in the light and air, outside. But we are in time. We "move with the times." That is, from His point of view, we move *away*, into what He regards as nonentity, where He never follows. That is all there is to us, all there ever was. He may be there in what you call "Life," or He may not (*P*, 168–69).

What we have is a very direct statement of the dangers of solipsism and anxiety over the ultimate solipsism, death. The "inside," which had seemed light and protecting in *Out of the Silent Planet* becomes in *Perelandra* dark and full of terror. The Weston that Ransom kills thus represents an aspect of himself, and Weston's death in the fiery abyss a symbol of Ransom's (and Lewis's) overcoming of solipsistic tendencies.

Ransom's reward is to witness the great cosmic dance, the sign of the true order of the universe (and of the order in himself): "It seemed to be woven out of the intertwining undulation of many cords or bands of light, leaping over and under one another and mutually embraced in arabesques and flower-like subtleties" (*P*, 218). Each figure within the dance seems to Ransom the motif which controls or organizes all the others, and yet as his attention shifts to a seeming detail the dance reorganizes itself in tune, in keeping with this new master motif. Ransom's vision is not unlike that of contemporary ecology, in which each individual and each group becomes meaningful in terms of its relationships to the complete set of groups and elements in the ecosystem.

Besides there being a test for Ransom, the novel describes the temptation of the woman, thereby introducing the theme of male-female relationships to Lewis's writing. But the curious thing is that her temptation is very similar to Ransom's. The Green Lady had been created as a helpmate to the King and the tempter obviously strikes out to subvert not only God's authority but also the King's. He does this by telling her stories of women who defied the wishes of their husbands to do great and noble deeds. Like Ransom, her temptation is to selfishness, but to a selfishness curiously involved with a perverted use of the imagination. The Green Lady resists the temptation, thus saving herself, Lewis tells us, from the fatal consequences of pride, that "fatal false step which, once taken, would thrust her down into the terrible slavery of appetite and hate and economics and government which our race knows so well" (*P,* 133).

Yet Lewis's solution is as static as the cosmic dance and as abstract as his description of it. If she is to be a "real woman" she must embody the archetype of femininity portrayed by the Oyarsa of Perelandra (Venus), just as Ransom, in order to be a "real man" must become like the masculine Malacandra.

> Malacandra seemed to him to have the look of one standing armed, at the ramparts of his own remote archaic world, in ceaseless vigilance, his eyes roaming the earthward horizon whence his danger came long ago. . . . But the eyes of Perelandra opened as it were, inward, as if they were the curtained gateway to a world of waves and murmurings and wandering airs, of life that rocked in winds and splashed on mossy stones and descended as the dew and arose sunward in thinspun delicacy of mist (*P,* 201).

The full description is much, much longer than this, but what we have here is enough to gauge Lewis's sense of the strong differentiation between the roles of men and those of women. He goes on in his description to endow these roles with all the meaning and significance of divine truth. "Nay," he tells us, if we can still find traces of these roles in human society today, it is because "in the very matter of our world, the traces of the celestial commonwealth are not quite lost" (*P,* 201). It would not be overharsh to label this position sexist. These stereotypes, which label men aggressive and domineering and women passive and receptive, are obviously only rationalizations of a social system which privileges men and oppresses women. It would be a mistake, however, to be overcritical of Lewis himself and to miss the main point of attack, the male chauvinist religion and society from which he inherits this polemic. What is more interesting about Lewis in this connection is that he feels, in order to discharge his responsibility to what he calls in his autobiography "the Other," that he has to deal with all this rigamarole about the sexes and their proper roles, when really he is not very interested in this at all (as his turn to children's stories indicates).

The only thing that saves the scene from being a simple diagram is the difficulty the eldils have in trying to accommodate their grandeur to the human eye; they're magnificent bunglers. "A tornado of sheer monstrosities seemed to be pouring over Ransom. Darting pillars filled with eyes, lightning pulsations of flame, talons and beaks and billowy masses of what suggested snow, volleyed through cubes and heptagons into an infinite black void. 'Stop it.... stop it,' Ransom yelled, with evident discomfort" (*P*, 197). Their second appearance is equally ill-considered. "Far off between the peaks on the other side of the little valley there came rolling wheels. there was nothing but that— concentric wheels moving with a rather sickening slowness one inside the other. There was nothing terrible about them if you could get used to their appalling size, but there was also nothing significant" (*P*, 198). They have to settle for a humanoid appearance.

Over all, the effect of *Perelandra* is much less satisfying than *Out of the Silent Planet*. For one thing, the editorial voice is stridently present:

> Weston was a man obsessed with the idea which is at this moment circulating all over our planet in obscure works of "scientifiction," in little Interplanetary Societies and Rocketry Clubs, and between the cover of monstrous magazines, ignored or mocked by the intellectuals, but ready, if ever the power is put into its hands, to open a new chapter of misery for the universe. It is the idea that humanity, having now sufficiently corrupted the planet where it arose, must at all costs contrive to seed itself over a larger area: that the vast astronomical distances which are God's quarantine regulations, must somehow be overcome. (*P*, 8).

By this device, he wants to let us into an orderly and generalizable universe. In the universe of this novel, it is such an author who guarantees us against the "Empirical Bogey." It might be tolerable in a work like the Narnia books, where the author is present consistently. But here, where it occurs only occasionally, it is a slip of control and evidence of Lewis's polemical reflex.

Consider also this passage on the splendors of the golden fruit of Perelandra:

> He had meant to extract the smallest, experimental sip, but the first taste put his caution all to flight. It was, of course, a taste, just as his thirst and hunger had been thirst and hunger. But then it was so different from every other taste that it seemed mere pedantry to call it a taste at all. It was like the discovery of a totally new *genus* of pleasures, something unheard of among men, out of all reckoning, beyond all covenant. (*P*, 42)

Of course, he wants to impress on us the planet's infinite goodness and variety. But isn't it a little too wonderful? He is so intent on telling us how different it is that he forgets to persuade us that it's real or that there's something in our ordinary sense experience which would lead us to want it.

An example of a related problem, not writing to the point, is displayed by this selection:

> As to conditions, well, I don't know much. It will be warm: I'm to go naked. Our astronomers don't know anything about the surface of Perelandra at all. The outer layer of her atmosphere is too thick. The main problem, apparently, is whether she revolves on her own axis or not, and at what speed. There are two schools of thought. There is a man called

Schiaparelli who thinks she revolves once on herself in the same time it takes her to go once around Arbol—I mean, the Sun. The other people think she revolves on her own axis once in every twenty-three hours. That's one of the things I shall find out (*P*, 26).

This is exactly the kind of thing that Lewis usually prefers to ignore in science fiction, technical details. He has no enthusiasm for technical details and it shows. His exposition is flat, listless, something to be hurried through. You can almost feel him straining to get at the excitement and exhileration of the giant seas and floating islands.

These problems are magnified in *That Hideous Strength*. *Perelandra* is too long. *That Hideous Strength* is as long as both previous novels combined. All the minor characters and incidents get in the way of themes that really interest Lewis—the contrasting moral failings of Mark and Jane Studdock and the contrast between St. Anne's and Belbury. Perhaps I should say they clarify too much. Mother Dimble, Camilla Denniston, and Ivy Maggs are all examples of the good wife and are contrasted with Jane as such. Likewise the men, Ransom, Denniston, and Dimble take their morality seriously even if it means foregoing social and material success. The static order, which squeezes the life out of the last part of *Perelandra*, overwhelms *That Hideous Strength* at many points.

Jane's failing is simply that she would be her own woman. She resents the demands Mark makes on her attentions and her body. Moreover, she thinks that she wants to continue her career, and consequently has persuaded Mark to practice contraception. She is bored with housekeeping and with her marriage, and sees it drifting to an inevitable breakup. But into this round of frustration and self-pity come her dreams and her power. She must decide whether she will use that power for her friends at St. Anne's and thus get drawn into something she can't control or whether she will keep the power to herself, try to ignore it, and let it rot away. As it turns out, she would not have been permitted the second alternative. The NICE at Belbury were ready to take her and exploit her for their own evil ends. Having given herself, however, to the company at St. Anne's, she discovers the reason for the failure of her marriage. Ransom tells her, "You do not fail in obedience through lack of love, but have lost love because you have never attempted obedience" (*THS*, 147). But only after a very severe warning—the vision of an unbaptized Venus, gross, sensual, and overwhelming—does she become a good wife to Mark. Ransom explains the vision to her: "And you, you know, are not a Christian wife. Neither are you a virgin. You have put yourself where you must meet with Old Woman and you have rejected all that has happened to her since Maledil came to earth. So you get her raw—not stronger than Mother Dimble would find her, but untransformed, demoniac. And you don't like it" (*THS*, 314). We find Jane, at the end of the novel, busily preparing a little honeymoon cottage for Mark's return. She has given up all thoughts of a career for herself and is ready to settle down and have children.

Jane, then, is acting the role that Lewis asigns his "baptized" Venus in *Perelandra*. It was unconvincing and unattractive there; here it is idiotic. To demand that a woman, especially a woman with intelligence and the willingness to use it, be no more than a housewife seems thoroughly benighted, even for Lewis's day and age. But it would be uncharitable if we did not also recognize that Jane is also a figure for Lewis, and that her submission imitates his own submission to Christian authority. Like Lewis, she would like to be "her own." Like Lewis, she has imaginative power. But she discovers that this power could become evil, unless she commits it to St. Anne's. To be meaningful, it has to be pitted against the evil at large in the world. We sense that in her figure Lewis is justifying his own commitment as a Christian polemicist.

Mark, on the other hand, is all too willing to let others do his thinking for him. He is the perfect organization man and an embodiment of that impulse to be "in" which Lewis detested so much at public school. He has no defenses when the NICE offer him power, money, prestige, even less when they threaten his life. He lies for them, he takes their snubs. He is, in Lewis's derisory term, "a spaniel." Yet once he comes close to death, he is able to review his life's sterility, and look at himself with unwonted clarity. "He had a picture of himself, the odious little outsider who wanted to be an insider, the infantile gull, drinking in the husky and unimportant confidences, as if he were being admitted to the government of the planet. Was there *no* beginning to his folly?" (*THS*, 245). As a result, he is prepared to die rather than sink further into perversion.

Ultimately he is received into the normative world of St. Anne's. St. Anne's is "Logres" (the Welsh name for Arthur's kingdom and a particular interest of Lewis's close friend Charles Williams). Logres is the real nation; all the rest is merely Britain:

> The poison was brewed in the West lands but it has spat itself everywhere by now. However far you went you would find the machines, the crowded cities, the empty thrones, the false writing, the barren beds: men maddened with false promises and soured with true miseries, worshipping the iron works of their own hands, cut off from Earth their mother and from the Father in heaven. You might go East so far that East became West and you returned to Britain across the great Ocean, but even so you would not have come out anywhere into the light. The shadow of one dark wing is over all Tellus. (*THS*, 293)

Only at St. Anne's are the men truly men, and the women truly women, according to the patterns set by Mars and Venus. St. Anne's is obviously an idealization of "the happy few" which had always been a part of Lewis's notion of society.

But as the quote above indicates, it is very small and very vulnerable. It is surrounded by a uniformly dark and threatening reality—the other permanent aspect of Lewis's notion of society. That other aspect is epitomized by Belbury. Everything at Belbury is a perversion. The Institute's chief policeman is a woman, a lesbian named "Fairy" Hardcastle. The chiefs of Belbury, Wither and Frost (what names!), carry on a strange homoerotic relationship. The program of the NICE is twofold—to terrorize, disrupt, and rule the common people and to win souls for the devil. For the first, a massive misuse of language is required. "Rehabilitation" becomes the word for the surgical and psychochemical manipulation of "honest criminals"; "eliminate red tape" the pretext for driving people from their homes and instituting martial law. That is why the word NICE is a little more than an artificial piece of irony. It signifies Lewis's pessimistic conviction that most people never give more thought to a situation than what people say about themselves. For the second purpose, initiates must be gathered to undergo a lengthy process of dehumanization. As the men and women of the NICE are parodies and perversions of "real men and women," so is the society of the Institute a vicious parody of a "real" society as exemplified in St. Anne's. It is the cruel, self-seeking society of Lewis's public school days: "Here was the world of plot within plot, crossing and double-crossing, of lies and graft and stabbing in the back, of murder and a contemptuous guffaw for the fool who lost the game" (*THS*, 245).

Most of the critics consider this novel by far the weakest in the trilogy. Undoubtedly part of the problem stems from the fact that Lewis shifts genres in mid-course; from a science-fiction adventure on the model of David Lindsay's *Voyage to Archturus,* he moves to a suspense-thriller modelled on John Buchan. As in the famous *Thirty-nine Steps,* we have two groups opposing one another, one dedicated to the preservation of England, the other to her destruction. Moreover, certain effects in *That Hideous Strength* are suggestive of those in a thriller. When Jane, walking along a foggy street, nearly walks right into Frost, the man who had been probing her mind for the NICE, or later when she is captured and in the clutches of the lesbian policewoman, we experience the same kind of terror as when Hannay walks unwittingly into the headquarters of the German spy ring. What is sorely missing in *That Hideous Strength* is the wonder and mystery which made up the greater part of the charm of the two earlier novels, yet it fails even as a thriller. Half the enjoyment in *The Thirty-nine Steps* is in watching Hannay outwit his enemies and thwart the German ploy. Lewis's heroes and heroines do nothing to stop the NICE's scheme. That is left to a *deus ex machina*—Merlin and a host of heavenly angels.

The real problem, however, is that the novel fails to solve the thematic concerns developing in the first two novels. The action of this novel shifts from the heavens to Earth, and we might reasonably expect that Ransom would put to use on Earth what he had learned in heaven. But this is not the case. The novel falls into two basically unrelated actions. Jane and Mark flee the NICE and join "the happy few" at St. Anne's; Merlin destroys the NICE. St. Anne's does nothing to destroy the threat at Belbury; this is why they look so rigid and why they talk so much. But the reason for this split is Lewis's own political despair. Ransom keeps his followers from attacking Belbury not because he is a coward, but because he knows that it will do no good. Even if they destroy Belbury, there is still all the rest of the world with "the shadow of one dark wing over all." Thus the image—light inside, dark outside—begun in *Out of the Silent Planet,* but reversed in that novel and *Perelandra,* again returns as the paradigm of reality. The only difference is that this time there are a few more people in the garden with Ransom.

4

C.S. Lewis: The Later Fantasies

Turning from *That Hideous Strength* to *The Lion, the Witch, and the Wardrobe*, the first in the series of Lewis's children's stories, one is struck by the tremendous change in tone. Lewis's great burst of polemical activity, which had begun in the 1930s and become so frenzied in the 1940s (twelve books in nine years), stopped somewhat abruptly in 1947. He did not return to deliberately apologetic writing until 1958 with *Reflections on the Psalms*. The tone of this work and of his last volumes of apologetics, *The Four Loves* (1960) and *A Grief Observed* (1961), an autobiographical account of the death of his wife and its shattering effect upon his religious faith, is much more subdued and tentative. It would probably be too much to say that Lewis completely lost interest in polemic after 1947. He was very busy after the war with the sudden influx of students into English studies. Clyde Kilby asserts that Lewis was probably the most popular tutor and lecturer at Oxford at that time. Perhaps, however, this sudden and dramatic display of interest in himself and his work took the edge off Lewis's sense of isolation. John Lawlor recounts that in the 1930s there were very few students at Oxford in Lewis's subject, English. As a result he often had to double as a tutor in a subject he absolutely hated, Political Science. Moreover, the few students he did get in English were "of very uneven quality." Most of them were simply unable to satisfy Lewis's demands for breadth of knowledge and intellectual rigor. But after the war, all that changed, and this seems to have had a pronounced effect on his writing.

The science-fiction trilogy is the work of a man battling with the world and with his imaginative materials. *The Lion, the Witch, and the Wardrobe*, on the other hand, is the work of a man completely at ease with himself and his materials. The violent and bloody fiasco of the banquet at Belbury, in which all the evil people are dispatched with considerable gore, and the pompous fertility ritual of the book's finale are left behind. Even the half-curious but still half-fearful encounter that Ransom has with the Martian, Hyoi, in *Out of the Silent Planet*, is too problematical for this new world. When little girls meet strange creatures in the wood here, they are not frightened:

He was only a little taller than Lucy herself and he carried over his head an umbrella, white with snow. From the waist upwards he was like a man, but his legs were shaped like a goat's (the hair on them was glossy black), and instead of feet he had goat's hoofs. He also had a tail, but Lucy did not notice this at first because it was neatly caught up over the arm that held the umbrella so as to keep it from trailing in the snow. He had a red woolen muffler round his neck and his skin was rather reddish too. He had a strange, but pleasant little face with a short pointed beard and curly hair, and out of the hair there stuck two horns, one on each side of his forehead. One of his two hands, as I have said, held the umbrella: in the other arm he carried several brown paper parcels. What with the parcels and the snow it looked just as if he had been doing his Christmas shopping. (*LWW*, 7–8)

What might have been signs of moral or sexual depravity for Ransom—the horns, the hooves, the tail—are here simply charming oddities. We are in a world very like Kenneth Grahame's, where people are odd, indeed, but oh so very interesting and friendly on the whole.

Nevertheless, there is a good deal of similarity between the two series of novels. First of all, the science fiction and the fairy tales both present visions of a glorified or beneficent "Nature." Both Malacandra and Narnia have talking animals, and there is a definite similarity in conception between the baptized mythological deities of Narnia (e.g., the fauns, satyrs, the tree and water spirits) and the guiding spirits of Malacandra and Perelandra, who besides being angels are identified as the classical Ares and Aphrodite. A second important similarity between the two works is the formation of a small society which believes in the other world. Finally, in both works Lewis is engaging in the translation of Christian mythology into a slightly different language, not so that it becomes unrecognizable but so that it gains freshness. As in the science fiction, this procedure sometimes works and sometimes doesn't. In Narnia, Christ is figured as a powerful golden-maned lion. Via what Kenneth Burke calls "perspective by incongruity," Lewis gains a new concreteness for Christ's power and his difference from ordinary humanity while at the same time reinforcing Lewis's reverence for nonhuman nature. A second example is the way Lewis tries to transform death. Just as Ransom joins Arthur on Perelandra, so the children do not lose Narnia by dying but rather gain access to the real, perfect Narnia.

It is this instance and this procedure which reveal Lewis's deep affinity with an earlier Christian writer of children's stories—a writer who had an important influence on Lewis's own spiritual development—George Macdonald. In Macdonald's *At the Back of the North Wind*, a little boy named Diamond meets a beautiful sad-faced lady named North Wind, who leads him to a country beyond the end of the known world. He discovers that it is a very pleasant place, if a little dull, and he stays there for a very long time. Eventually, he returns home, like Dorothy in Oz, by waking from a serious illness, and discovers that he has been away only a little while. He has more interviews and adventures with North Wind until she reveals her other name, the name most people know her by, Death. But by then Diamond is not at all afraid of her and consequently not afraid of dying. When he does die, he goes with her joyfully and finds a place even better than the first place, which was only a picture or reflection of the Real Thing, a place so good that the author simply can't describe it for us. Here he hints not only of the time displacement, important to the relationship between Narnia and Earth, but also of the many Narnias, each more beautiful than the next, which become important to Lewis's teleology.

So much for the similarities. The differences are crucial in establishing the greater consistency and sureness of tone which assure Narnia's being an artistically more successful work. First and foremost is the difference in genre. Whereas the science fiction trilogy contains many elements of the realistic and psychological traditions of novel writing, e.g., love interest and close psychology, the fairy stories do not. This characteristic is no doubt due to the basic materials from which they sprang. The fairy stories began as a group of images, e.g., a faun carrying an umbrella, a queen on a sledge, a wonderful lion, which eventually arranged themselves into a series of events. These images seemed to demand the kind of treatment one finds in a fairy tale, a kind of treatment which precluded many of the ailments which Lewis's earlier fiction fell victim to: "analysis, digression, reflections, and 'gas'" (*OOW*, 37). Thus, Lewis seems to have learned that an ordinary novel such as *That Hideous Strength* was capable of getting out of control in his hands. Sexual and social relations drop out of the picture; what remains is a picture of the democracy of childhood, after the model of E. Nesbit's stories. What also drops out are the epistemological difficulties Ransom experienced in *Out of the Silent Planet*. In Narnia good and evil are readily apparent. Those who do not see evil are evil themselves and know it deep down. It is a situation very much like that of *The Wind in the Willows* where all right-thinking animals know that weasels and stoats are a bad lot. Ransom's philological enthusiasms are left out as well, and we are left with heroes and heroines whose major concerns are mundane ones of food, play, affection, adventure, and beauty.

Lewis wants to draw people to Christ by creating a world in which the gratification of natural desires leads to a desire for the "Ultimate Good." His confidence that men's natural desires will eventually lead them to Christ allows him to eschew the dogmatism which had previously weighed his work down. He no longer has to tell us that human affection if rightly ordered will lead us to Christ; he shows us Lucy and Susan fussing over, rubbing, and playing with Aslan. There is less doctrine and more morality; fewer imitations of medieval religion (and those better assimilated) and more day-to-day interaction between ordinary children.

All these factors contribute to the greater simplicity and cheerfulness of Narnia. There are other factors which, though they look at first as if they're going to complicate things, actually enhance the simplicity. The first of these changes is the addition of the narrator as a permanent fact of the fiction. This actually simplifies the emotional response of reading because it gives the reader "authoritative" cues as to what's going on in the scene and as to the proper mode of response. How are we to respond to the evil Queen's gift of "Turkish Delight" for which Edmund develops such a craving? We are suitably dismayed when the narrator tells us that "this was enchanted Turkish Delight and that anyone who had once tasted it would want more and more of it, and would even, if they were allowed, go on eating it till they killed themselves" (*LWW*, 33). The narrator, safe, sane, and friendly person that he is, is the author's guarantee that nothing irrational or violent is going to frighten us more than we can bear.

The second factor, which though complicating the fiction, enhances the effect of simplicity, is the time differential between Earth and Narnia. Time goes by much more quickly in Narnia than on Earth. The whole cycle from creation to apocalypse—many thousands of years—takes place in two or three generations on Earth. Thus when once the children leave Narnia they never know what to expect when they return. In one instance, a young Narnian friend has grown old in the interval and is about to die. But feelings of loss are mitigated quite simply by the continued existence of the characters from Earth. They, like the reader, survive quite nicely the various shocks the flesh is heir to. Moreover, the Wellsian vision of death and detritus is rebutted; Narnia does not simply end—it becomes the gateway to a new glorified Narnia. With this particular dramatic device, Lewis has captured quite nicely a sense of the soul's desire for transcendence in the face of the passing of material things, and assured his readers of the friendliness of Narnia and the attractiveness of his world view.

The one complicating factor in this cunningly simple world is the presence of evil, both physical and moral. In the science-fiction trilogy the glorified planets of Mars and Venus are proposed mainly as contrasts to the evil condition of Earth. The presence of evil on either one is an "intolerable obscenity." Evil has been present in Narnia, however, ever since the hour of its creation. Like Earth it is a fallen world. But it still has magic. It is like Lewis's vision of Earth before the death of Merlin, "an era in which the general relations of mind and matter on this planet had been other than those we know" (*THS*, 201). It was a world in which the fields, the forests, the rivers, the wild animals still spoke to and obeyed man.

So much for the relation of the stories to the science-fiction trilogy. As to the general drift of the stories themselves, the first four concern the founding of the relationship between Earth and Narnia and the building of the company of Narnia. The next two involve mainly the extension of the Narnian world in space and time. We remember Lewis's enthusiasm for fictional works which create whole worlds of wonders. In the final volume, we have the end of both

Narnia and the company of Narnia—or, as Lewis would have it, their beginning. The fallen Narnia of their earlier experience is replaced by the glorified Narnia of their desire.

The Lion, the Witch, and the Wardrobe, the first of the stories, is one of the most charming of the group. It is the story of four children, Peter, Susan, Edmund, and Lucy Pevensy, staying at an old professor's house in the country during the London blitz. It is a very large house and on rainy days the children play exciting games of hide and seek. Once during such a game, Lucy, the youngest of the children, hides in a wardrobe full of fur coats and as she moves toward the back finds she is in a snow-covered forest. She meets the Faun, Tumnus, who inivites her to his cave for a gorgeous snack. The light and cheerful tone of these first moments in Narnia is suddenly undercut, however, for Tumnus shamefacedly explains that he has been a villain and that he had intended to kidnap Lucy for the White Witch. He repents though and leads her back to the forest. When she gets out of the wardrobe not two minutes after she had gotten in, she runs to tell the others of her adventure. But they don't believe her.

Another time both Lucy and Edmund, the second youngest, get into Narnia through the wardrobe. Edmund meets the White Witch and, enchanted by her magic candy, promises to bring the others to her. (The witch fears that these are the four human children who are prophecied to end her rule.) Finally all four children enter Narnia and meet some friendly animals who warn them against the witch. While eating dinner with beavers, Edmund, hungry for the candy and the power which the witch has promised him over the other children, slips away to tell her that the others are in Narnia. They soon discover his treachery and set off for the hill of the Stone Table, where they hope to meet Aslan, son of "The Emperor Across the Sea," who is the best chance for defeating the witch. As they rush to meet him, the winter that had settled over the land for a hundred years suddenly dissolves into a magical spring. They meet Aslan and rescue Edmund. But the witch demands her right as stated in "the deep Magic from the Dawn of Time"—the traitor must die. Aslan takes Edmund's place and the witch kills him. Lucy and her sister Susan come to mourn their dead friend, but at dawn he comes alive again. He frees the witch's victims from their marble state and leads them to where Peter and Edmund and the Talking Beasts under their command are fighting the witch's army. With the arrival of Aslan and reinforcements, the battle is soon over, the witch is killed, and the children are installed as kings and queens of Narnia. Their reign is the Golden Age.

The marvelous quality of this particular story—and of other of the Narnia books—is its lightness and cheerfulness of tone. We have already met with sprightly figure Tumnus. Equally engaging is the wonderful tea he prepares for himself and Lucy:

And really it was a wonderful tea. There was a nice brown egg, lightly boiled, for each of them, and then sardines on toast, and then buttered toast, and then toast with honey, and then a sugar-topped cake. And when Lucy was tired of eating the Faun began to talk. He had wonderful tales to tell of life in the forest. He told about the midnight dances and how the Nymphs who lived in the wells and the Drayds who lived in the trees came out to dance with the Fauns: about long hunting parties after the milk-white Stag who could give you wishes if you caught him; about feasting and treasure-seeking with the wild Red Dwarfs in deep mines and caverns far beneath the forest floor; and then about summer when the woods were green and old Silenus on his fat donkey would come to visit them, and sometimes Bacchus himself, and then the streams would run with wine instead of water and the whole forest would give itself up to jollification for weeks on end. (*LWW*, 13)

Good stories and good food, Lewis tells us in an essay called "Three Ways of Writing for Children," have always been things which he enjoyed, not only as a child, but as an adult, and his own zest for these things enters his writing. You cannot write down to children and please them, he says; you must write about experiences and joys you have in common with them. Lewis's enjoyment of the simple pleasures of childhood is found throughout the novel. For example, when Aslan frees the animals, who had been turned into statues by the witch, the result is a riot of color and sound:

Instead of all that deadly white the courtyard was now a blaze of colours; glossy chestnut side of centaurs, indigo horns of unicorns, dazzling plumage of birds, reddy-brown of foxes, dogs, and satyrs, yellow stockings and crimson hoods of dwarfs; and the birch-girls in silver, and the beech-girls in fresh, transparent green, and the larch-girls in green so bright that it was almost yellow. And instead of the deadly silence the whole place rang with the sound of happy roarings, brayings, yelpings, barkings, squealings, cooings, neighings, stampings, shouts, hurrahs, songs and laughter. (*LWW*, 166)

There is enthusiasm for nature in this passage, but also a joy in the language too. This is very good writing. Though the syntax is simple, there is a fullness of presentation and a subtle strangeness in the vocabulary (centaur, indigo, unicorn, satyr) which makes it memorable.

As we move into Narnia with Lucy we feel that we have moved into something strange and exciting but not unfriendly. "Lucy felt frightened, but she felt very inquisitive and excited as well. She looked back over her shoulder and there, between the dark tree-trunks, she could still see the open door way of the wardrobe and even catch a glimpse of the empty room from which she had set out" (*LWW*, 7). There is something very cozy about moving from a closet of furs into a forest of firs. There is little of the fear that haunts John (in *Pilgrim's Regress*) or Weston (in *Perelandra*) or Orual (in *Till We Have Faces*), that we will disappear down a black hole never to return. Likewise, Lewis seems to have made peace with his imagination and accepted its fantasies. These stories betray no fear of the moral evil of subjectivism or the psychological danger of solopsism. The imaginary world, though a limited good, is accepted and enjoyed as such.

This is much the same attitude as that of E. Nesbit, whose children's stories Lewis admired very much. In fact, the original situation of *The Lion, the Witch, and the Wardrobe* is similar to that of many of her stories—ordinary children on vacation look for adventure and find it. Also like Nesbit, Lewis concentrates on the ethical qualities of the children's life together.

Some of the other really good touches also take us back into the best of English children's books. The beavers' nest reminds us of the coziness of Mole's home in *Wind in the Willows*: "There were no books or pictures and instead of beds there were bunks, like on board ship, built into the wall. And there were hams and strings of onions hanging from the roof and against the walls were gum boots and oilskins and hatchets and pairs of shears and spades and trowels and things for carrying mortar in and fishing rods and fishing nets and sacks. And the cloth on the table tho' very clean was very rough" (*LWW*, 69).

Other touches are Lewis's own. We remember his fondness for classical and Christian images in the science-fiction trilogy (where the pagan gods Ares and Aphrodite become the angels who guide Mars and Venus in their spheres), and we notice that the White Witch is a gorgon. She turns her unruly subjects into statues. But she is also a devil, and one of Lewis's most evil creations.

Even more characteristic and effective is the incident in which the witch changes into a boulder to escape Edmund's rescuers. When the narrator remarks that "she could make things look like what they weren't," we are reminded of Lewis's concern with metaphors of blindness. We feel we are looking at the real witch, something cold, hard, and desolate. But also the irony of the gorgon's changing herself into stone is delicious.

Another touch equally characteristic of Lewis is his description of the Stone Table. "It was a great grim slab of grey stone supported on four upright stones. It looked very old; and it was cut all over with strange lines and figures that might be the letters of an unknown language. They gave you a curious feeling when you looked at them" (*LWW*, 121–22). This is deliberately vague, filled with suggestions of weird rites, of unimaginable cruelty, of immemorial and iniquitous antiquity.

A final touch that signs the book as Lewis's own is the contrast of spring and winter. The witch is queen of winter. With her dead white face, she reminds us of Wither in *That Hideous Strength*. But the Lion brings spring, not only in the spiritual sense but also to remind us that he is the author of all the good we receive from nature. We experience something of Lewis's own joy in nature in the description of that sudden spring. It is an exact parallel of Lewis's description of his own re-admittance to the company of "Joy" when an adolescent.

Lewis's description of the Golden Age in Narnia reminds us of the deep strain of anarchism that resides on English children's literature. "They made good laws and kept the peace and saved good trees from being unnecessarily cut down, and liberated young dwarfs and young satyrs from being sent to school, and generally stopped busybodies and interferers and encouraged ordinary people who wanted to live and let live" (*LWW*, 180). Nesbit's *Five Children and It* and Barrie's *Peter Pan* are other stories in which the attempt of children to escape a world run by adults is seen as wholesome and healthy. But it is even more of an achievement for a man like Lewis, who has spent his whole working life in school, and is able to suddenly "liberate young dwarfs and young satyrs from being sent to school."

One of the few elements of the story which remind us of the more unfortunate aspects of Lewis's opinions are his insistence that while it is unnatural for girls to fight, it is wholly fitting and heroic for boys.

Moreover, the murder of Aslan and the subsequent events are almost too close a parallel with the crucifixion and resurrection of Christ. We even get the rending of the temple veil and the women at the Tomb. In fact, the last section of the book, from the meeting with Aslan on, doesn't have the same quality of imagination as the first half. The parallels with Christian myth take over the story and pin down the meaning too specifically (something for which there is much precedent in Lewis's career). For example, as soon as the Stone Table becomes more than a symbol of a rich, wild, and barbaric past and becomes the Old Covenant, the magic of the story fades. The pathos of Aslan's death is forced, for what we are viewing is a ritual reenactment, the Mass, and not an imagined event. During her debate with the Lion, the witch says, "You know that every traitor belongs to me as my lawful prey and that for every treachery I have a right to a kill" (*LWW*, 139). This is "the Deep Magic from the Dawn of Time." But it is also a translation of the terms of the Old Testament, "an eye for an eye." To supersede it we have the "Deeper Magic from before the Dawn of Time," in which the innocent Aslan substitutes for the traitor Edmund. Aslan says, " If the witch could have looked into the stillness and darkness before Time dawned, she would have known that when a willing victim who had committed no treachery was killed in a traitor's stead, the Table would crack and Death itself would start working backwards" (*LWW*, 160). This is also a simple translation of the New Covenant inaugurated by the death of Christ. Not only is the sequence lacking in imaginative power, it is almost an ad hoc addition to the story of the little girl and the faun. As Lewis had once said, "Once you get your characters to the other world, they have to do something," and all Lewis could think to do with them was to let them observe a reenactment of the central Christian dogma. In fact, this concept of the "Deep Magic" does not appear in the later stories and is not mentioned at all in the story in which we learn of the origins of the White Witch, *The Magician's Nephew*.

The central event of the first book is Aslan's sacrifice, the central virtue, self-sacrifice. The second book, *Prince Caspian*, a straightforward adventure story, is equally clear. The key event is the restoration of Prince Caspian to his throne and the central virtue is reverence for nature and tradition. The story is this: Caspian's throne is usurped by his uncle Miraz, who is a cruel and tyrannical ruler. Not only does he line his pockets with his people's hard-earned money, he is also engaged in a vicious campaign to eradicate all memory and trace of Old Narnia, the dwarfs, talking beasts and trees. But he is not the first to pursue this impious policy. He belongs to a race, the Tellmarines, who settled Narnia after the Golden Age and sought to exterminate the natives. Caspian, however, because of the wonderful stories his nurse and tutor tell him of Old Narnia, longs to meet these strange creatures. When his uncle has a son, Caspian, the true heir, is in danger of his life. He flees to the forest where he is befriended by Old Narnia. The Tellmarines attack the Narnians and Caspian, in desparate straits, blows the magic horn of Queen Susan. Help arrives in the form of Aslan and the four children from Earth. While Aslan gathers reinforcements, Peter challenges Miraz to single combat; but there is treachery in the enemy ranks. Miraz is killed by one of his own men. The Tellmarines set upon the embattled Narnians but Aslan arrives in time with an army of trees and the day is saved. Aslan makes a door in the air and those Tellmarines unhappy with Narnia return to Earth, their original home. Others, mostly young ones, stay. Old Narnia once more takes its rightful place in society and at the councils of the king, and the children return home.

The basic theme reminds us, of course, of certain elements of *That Hideous Strength*, where the holy hush of Bracton Wood was destroyed by the bulldozers of NICE and where vast armies of unfeeling technicians performed experiments on animals and criminals. In this book, however, where the tone isn't quite so shrill, Lewis is much more successful in persuading us of the value and the integrity of nature. In the first place, tradition is living, and it is a group of creatures with a peculiarly charming and quaint way of life. Moreover, we can respect the integrity of nature because nature, in the persons of the various Talking Beasts, is so obviously stamped with character. Reepicheep, the mouse with the heart—and mouth—of a lion, is the foremost example. He is a splendid and dashing fellow. "He was of course bigger than a common mouse, well over a foot high when he stood on his hind legs, and with ears nearly as long as (though broader than) a rabbit's.... He wore a tiny little rapier at his side and twirled his long whiskers as if they were a moustache. 'There are twelve of us, Sir,' he said with a dashing and graceful bow, 'and I place all the resources of my people unreservedly at your Majesty's disposal'"(*PC*, 75). Or consider the courtesy of the three "bulgy" bears:

> There was a noise like a small earthquake from inside and a sort of door opened and out came three brown bears, very bulgy indeed and blinking their little eyes. And when everything had been explained to them, (which took a long time because they were so sleepy) they said that a Son of Adam ought to be King of Narnia and all kissed Caspian—very wet, snuffly kisses they were—and offered him some honey. Caspian did not really want honey, without bread, at that time in the morning, but he thought it polite to accept. It took him a long time afterwards to get unsticky. (*PC*, 69)

As we have already seen in *The Lion, the Witch, and the Wardrobe*, Narnia is a much happier place than fairy worlds of the science-fiction trilogy. The tunes in *Perelandra* are so solemn. But listen to the pipe music of this passage. We meet

> a youth, dressed only in a fawn-skin, with vine leaves wreathed in his curly hair. His face would have been almost too pretty for a boy's, if it had not looked so extremely wild. You felt, as Edmund said when he saw him a few days later, "There's a chap who might do anything—absolutely anything." He seemed to have a great many names—Bromios, Bassareus, and the Ram, were three of them. There were a lot of girls with him, as wild as he. There was even, unexpectedly, someone on a donkey. And everybody was laughing: and everybody was shouting out, "Euan, euan, eu-oi-oi-oi."
>
> "Is it a Romp, Aslan?" cried the youth. And apparently it was. But nearly everyone seemed to have a different idea as to what they were playing. It may have been Tig, but Lucy never discovered who was It. It was rather like Blind Man's Bluff, only everyone behaved as if he was blindfolded. It was not unlike Hunt the Slipper, but the slipper was never found. What made it more complicated was that the man on the donkey, who was old and enormously fat, began calling out at once, "Refreshments! Time for refreshments," and falling off his donkey and being bundled on to it again by the others, while the donkey was under the impression that the whole thing was a circus, and tried to give a display of walking on its hind legs. And all the time there were more and more vineleaves everywhere! And soon not only leaves but vines. They were climbing up everything. They were running up the legs of the tree people and circling round their necks. Lucy put up her hands to push back her hair and found she was pushing back vine branches. The donkey was a mass of them. His tail was completely entangled and something dark was nodding between his ears. Lucy looked again and saw it was a bunch of grapes. After that it was mostly grapes—overhead and underfoot and all around. (*PC*, 152–53)

I hope I may be forgiven for quoting such a lengthy passage, but this is one of the best passages in all of Lewis's writing and deserves attention. Obviously he leaves a lot of the classical conception of Bacchus—drunkenness and violence—out of this description, but a lot of bacchic spirit has been infused into Lewis's Christianity. I don't think that anywhere else has Lewis so deftly mobilized classical myth on behalf of his own feeling for nature and for physical enjoyment. His Ares and Aphrodite are wooden puppets by comparison. Only his unbaptized Venus in *That Hideous Strength* displays a similar energy and strength of conception.

There is an unwonted joy in this world and a new attitude to physical indulgence. Drinking in *That Hideous Strength* is quite simply a sign of moral depravity, as when Mark repeatedly blinds himself to the evil of his situation and actions with alcohol. In other places, the drinking of wine is almost a sacramental action, as when Ransom (and later the magician in *Voyage of the Dawn Treader*) lives on a diet of bread and wine. Here it is one of the good things of life.

Even his villains are better. Consider, for instance, the "dull, grey voice" of the werewolf: "I'm hunger. I'm thirst, Where I bite, I hold till I die, and even after death they must cut out my mouthful from my enemy's body and bury it with me. I can fast a hundred years and not die. I can lie a hundred nights on the ice and not freeze. I can drink a river of blood and not burst. Show me your enemies" (*PC*, 160). That will scare almost anybody. But we notice also the care in the writing, the careful grouping of sibilants and long 'i' sounds that give the passage a spooky feeling. Lewis is very successful at giving this villain a distinctive voice.

The joy of the Bacchus passage carries over into the rest of the book. At the restoration of Old Narnia, the company interrupts a Tellmarine schoolroom, and one of the children decides to come with them. "Instantly she joined hands with two of the Maenads who whirled her round in a merry dance and helped her take off some of the unnecessary and uncomfortable clothes that she was wearing" (*PC*, 195).

We remember that during the Golden Age the High King Peter had let young dwarfs and fauns out of school. In fact, Lewis's attitude throughout this book seems to be generally opposed to school. The book begins with the four children glumly waiting to go back to school and ends with the observation that "It was odd, and not very nice, to take off their royal clothes and to put on their school things" (*PC*, 215). Obviously, we should feel here Lewis's animus against the schools of his own youth. Here, as everywhere else in the Narnia books, the fantasy world, the world of childhood, is superior to the world run by adults.

With *The Voyage of the Dawn Treader* we begin to feel that the impetus that first created Narnia is dying out. There is a good deal of satire—nice but irrelevant to the purposes of a fairy tale—at the expense of an Eustace Scrubb, a new member of the company, and his up-to-date parents and school. More importantly there is the absence of a central action as well as a central theme to guide the progress of the book. King Caspian has sworn to go in search of the seven nobles—the last of those loyal to himself and his father—sent by Miraz on a journey in the Eastern Sea to find the end of the world. Obviously the image of voyaging among islands is very significant for Lewis—it is the one he uses to describe his life after his mother's death. It is also a very odd image for a spiritual quest. In Donne's "Easter Morning—Travelling Westward" the movement away from the rising sun is a sign of alienation from God, just as Lewis's movement toward the orient sun is a movement toward God. It is not irrelevant in this context that George Macdonald's hero in *The Phantastes* travels in a generally easterly direction. But we are never sure whether the central action of the novel is the search for the lost nobles or one of the adventures on the way or the very act of voyaging toward the end of the world.

No controlling value is clearly emphasized. Is it Caspian's faithfulness to his promise to seek out the seven lords? Is it Reepicheep's noble daring as he sails over the edge of the world? Is it Caspian's devotion to duty and his country as he turns back from following Reepicheep? We just can't tell. There are too many loose ends.

Nor are the episodes equally good. Eustace's stint as a dragon is good, especially his discovery of his plight. He finds a dead dragon and its hoard of gold, and he falls asleep on top of the hoard. When he awakes, he notices an ominous presence in the cave with him.

> He moved his right arm in order to feel his left, but stopped before he had moved it an inch and bit his lip in terror. For just in front of him, and a little on his right, where the moonlight fell clear on the floor of the cave, he saw a hideous shape moving. He knew the shape: it was a dragon's claw. It had moved as he moved his hand and became still when he stopped moving his hand. (*VDT*, 73)

At first he thinks it is the dead dragon's mate, but then he realizes the truth. "Sleeping on a dragon's hoard with greedy, dragonish thoughts in his heart, he had become a dragon himself" (*VDT*, 75) The discovery that what had seemed an objective menace was really only his own foul subjectivity is a worthy invention of Lewis's ethical imagination. Good also is the fact that Eustace makes the best of his condition—he fells timber for the repair of the ship and scavenges food for the crew.

Then there is the moment of imaginative clarity when the fantasy world develops according to its own demands—as Lewis in his essay "Of Science Fiction" had seen that it must. Lucy spies an undersea kingdom, with its own fields, flocks, and castles. What puzzles her, however, is why they build their castles on mountaintops instead of in the valleys like sensible folk. The reason is astoundingly simple:

> In the sea, the deeper you go, the darker and colder it gets, and it is down there, in the dark and cold, that dangerous things live—the squid and the Sea Serpent and the Kraken. The valleys are the wild, unfriendly places. The sea-people feel about their valleys as we do about mountains, and feel about their mountains as we feel about valleys. It is on the heights (or, as we would say, "in the shallows") that there is warmth and peace. The reckless hunters and brave knights of the sea go down into the depths on quests and adventures, but return home to the heights for rest and peace, courtesy and council, the sports, the dances and the songs. (*VDT*, 193)

This is exactly what Lewis meant when he talked of "the intellect, almost completely free from emotion, at play." His interest in fully developed imaginary worlds, constructed on an impossible hypothesis, is caught here in microcosm.

By contrast with these two episodes, the episode of the Dark Island is not nearly so effective. But Lewis tries to make it harrowing. The voyagers discover a cloud of darkness on the sea, which they enter and which completely blots out the rays of the sun.

How long this voyage into the darkness lasted, nobody knew. Except for the creak of the rowlocks and the splash of the oars there was nothing to show that they were moving at all. Edmund, peering from the bows, could see nothing except the reflection of the lantern in the water before him. It looked a greasy sort of reflection, and the ripple made by their advancing prow appeared to be heavy, small and lifeless. As time went on everyone except the rowers began to shiver with cold. (*VDT*, 154)

Eventually they are discovered by a castaway who tells them, "This is the island where dreams come true." And of course this is just the pretext for Lewis, the Christian polemicist, to plumb the depths of human depravity. "It had taken everyone just that half-minute to remember certain dreams they had had— dreams that make you afraid of going to sleep again—and to realize what it would mean to land on a country where dreams come true" (*VDT*, 157). Immediately the rowers row backwards, hoping against hope that they will escape the Dark Island. Finally they pull out of the darkness and away from the island. Who isn't afraid of the dark, when asked to remember his nightmares? But, as can be detected from the abstractness and generality of the quotation, the incident as a whole remains a sketch for an episode rather than a fully developed creation.

The incident with the Duffers is in many ways very picturesque. They have only one foot and must hop around. (They are derived from the medieval tradition of Unipeds, who live near the equator and use their giant foot as a shield against the fierce noonday sun.) Also the Duffers are invisible. Dinner with the Duffers is a very interesting experience indeed.

It was very funny to see the plates and dishes coming to the table and not to see anyone carrying them. It would have been funny even if they had moved along level with the floor, as you would expect things to do in invisible hands. But they didn't. They progressed up the long dining-hall in a series of bounds and jumps. At the highest point of each jump a dish would be about fifteen feet up in the air; then it would come down and stop quite suddenly about three feet from the floor. When the dish contained anything like soup or stew the result was rather disastrous. (*VDT*, 123)

Also they have the most curious conversational style:

Indeed most of their remarks were the sort it would not be easy to disagree with: "What I always say is, when a chap's hungry, he likes some victuals," or "Getting dark now; always does at night," or even "Ah, you've come over the water. Powerful wet stuff, ain't it?" (*VDT*, 124)

The problem is that Lucy and the other crew members who have been captured by the Duffers are threatened with a type of violence unheard of so far in

Narnia, not the heroic violence of war but the cowardly violence of brigands and slaves. It is not a struggle between equals but an unfeeling victimization of the innocent. The Duffers explain that they have been changed into monopods by the evil magician who rules their island. Disgusted with their appearance, they send their Chief's daughter into the magician's room to find the right spell which will make them invisible. Eventually they get tired of being invisible and want to change back, but now they are afraid to send one of their own children to do the deed. The magician also has been made invisible by their spell and only waits, they fear, for another such attempt to unleash his magic against them. Consequently they wait until they can kidnap a stranger like Lucy, whom they can terrorize into doing their will. Fortunately Lucy discovers that the magician is really a servant of Aslan and that he has been set over the Duffers for their own good. They are not evil in themselves, but their opportunism leads them into cruel and treacherous actions. In this regard, they are the forerunners of the evil dwarfs of Book 7.

The episode of Deathwater Island is a morality play that is neither fully developed nor motivated. Caspian, Edmund and Lucy come upon a lake where everything that touched the water turns to gold. Caspian is suddenly seized with the impulse to claim it for Narnia and threatens the others if they reveal its location. The boys draw their swords against one another, but suddenly Aslan appears. The curse is lifted and they row away chastened. What's disturbing is that it is completely out of character for the noble Caspian and the ennobled Edmund.

Similarly, the stars whom the travelers meet at "the beginning of the end of the world" are conceptual cousins of the Ares and Aphrodite of *Perelandra* but without their redeeming ineptness. "It was like an old man. His silver beard came down to his bare feet in front and his silver hair hung down to his heels behind and his robe appeared to be made from the fleece of silver sheep. He looked so mild and grave that once more all the travelers rose to their feet and stood in silence" (*VDT*, 176).

In many ways, *The Voyage of the Dawn Treader* is the weakest of the Narnia stories. The next book, *The Silver Chair*, although not up to the excellence of *Prince Caspian*, nevertheless represents a definite recovery of narrative control. The central event is the rescue of Caspian's son Prince Rilian from the enchantment of an evil witch. There is a strong secondary plot in which Eustace and his schoolmate Jill Pole, after effecting Rilian's rescue, return to their school with Aslan and chasten the school bullies who had made their life so miserable. It is interesting to note that this is the same pattern as in the trilogy where Ransom travels to a strange world and returns with powers who will chastise the enemies of God. The central moral event of this novel is Jill's faithfulness to Aslan's commands.

The first thing one notices is that the tone of the book has changed from the earlier works. Life is getting much harder, much more strenuous in Narnia. This has something to do, of course, with the fact that for the first time in the series, Aslan is little more than a minor character. He appears at the beginning to give Jill her instructions and at the end to lead her back to school, but the adventure is almost entirely her own responsibility. Only once does he show up to help her and that in a dream. Also Lewis seems now to distrust what had earlier been one of his major tools for attracting his audience, the excitement of adventure. Lucy is able to indulge her love of adventure quite licitly in *Prince Caspian*. But a similar taste is completely out of place for Jill. She is criticized for being a callow little schoolgirl and not realizing that duty is duty regardless of whether the adventure is exciting or just plain difficult. The four Pevensies ride to adventure in complete comfort, or at most slight discomfort. Eustace and Jill set out in the midst of winter on a journey that takes many days of walking in endless cold, sleeping on rocky ground, catching their meals as they can. Self-indulgence of the most innocent kind—hot food and a warm bed—almost spells disaster when, seeking food and lodging at a giant's castle, they are instead put on the menu. Obviously Lewis wants to wean his audience from a taste for mere adventure and in this book his morality is becoming more rigorous and adult.

The prospect, however, is by no means completely grim. Despite their mistakes and their lapses in duty, they finally accomplish their task and return home to round out their triumph over evil. Even the journey itself is not so bad. The tedium and the danger are relieved by the presence of their guide, one of Lewis's most original and loveable characters, Puddleglum, the Marshwiggle. Now the Marshwiggles are serious folk and given to the most pessimistic observations. After comfortably settling the children in his wigwam, he says, "There you are. Best we can do. You'll lie cold and hard. Damp too, I shouldn't wonder. Won't sleep a wink, most likely; even if there isn't a thunderstorm or a flood or the wigwam doesn't fall down on top of us all, as I've known them to do. Must make the best of it—" (*SC*, 56). But balancing this pessimistic bias in his character is an unexampled kindness, generosity, resourcefulness, and bravery. Puddleglum leads them through the dangerous land of the giants, feeds them, and saves them from the witch's enchantment by thrusting his foot in a fire. Nor is he a complete wet blanket. When things seem blackest to Pole, when they're prisoners of the witch's gnomes, he reminds her, "Now don't you let your spirits down, Pole. . . . There's one thing you've got to remember. We're back on the right lines. We were to go under the Ruined City, and we *are* under it. We're following the instructions again" (*SC*, 128). Yet his seriousness is more than something to laugh at. Beside it, the laughter of the enchanted prince is shallow and foolish. The prince's description of the invasion of the uplands which the witch is preparing is what tips Jill off that something is wrong with him.

> But fie on gravity! Is it not the most comical and ridiculous thing in the world to think of them all going about their business and never dreaming that under their peaceful fields and floors, only a fathom down, there is a great army ready to break out upon them like a fountain! And they never to have suspected! Why, they themselves, when once the first smart of their defeat is over, can hardly choose but laugh at the thought! (*SC*, 138)

Nor is the book without real adventure. (As Lewis would say, if you keep secondary things in their proper place, you get to keep them.) After they escape from the giants' castle, they are captured by the witch's army. The journey in the Underworld in the kingdom of the witch, however, succeeds where the episode of the Dark Island does not. The darkness becomes smothering and suffocating in a very convincing way. Jill knows what it is all about.

> She hated dark, underground places. And when, as they went on, the cave got lower and narrower, and when, at last, the light-bearer stood aside, and the gnomes, one by one, stooped down (all except the very smallest ones) and stepped into a little dark crack and disappeared, she felt she could bear it no longer. "I can't go in there, I can't! I can't! I won't," she panted. (*SC*, 124)

Lewis is evoking our animal fear of death and yoking it with his own hatred of evil. Particularly effective in recreating this deadening of the spirit is their journey on the underground sea.

> When they woke, everything was just the same; the gnomes still rowing, the ship still gliding on, still dead blackness ahead. How often they woke and slept and ate and slept again, none of them could ever remember. And the worst thing about it was that you began to feel as if you had always lived on that ship, in that darkness, and to wonder whether sun and blue skies and wind and birds had not been only a dream. (*SC*, 128)

This is obviously an expansion of the Dark Island episode in Book 3. But here it works much better and we can believe the final sentence. Here it is prepared for, becomes part of a major structure of images and thought. There it was just a blot out of the blue. Further enhancing the effect is the description of the Dark City:

> It was a queer city. The lights were so few and far apart that they would hardly have done for scattered cottages in our world. But the little bits of the place which you could see by the lights were like glimpses of a great sea-port. You could make out in one place a whole crowd of ships loading or unloading; in another, bales of stuff and warehouses; in a third, walls and pillars that suggested great palaces or temples; and always, wherever the light fell, endless crowds—.... but there was not a song or a shout or a bell or the rattle of a wheel anywhere. The City was as quiet, and nearly as dark, as the inside of an ant-hill. (*SC*, 129)

This might be London in a fog or one of the industrial cities.

It seems to owe something to Baudelaire and Eliot. But this city has an important economic dimension. The gnomes are enchanted too and work for the witch only because they are forced. It is only when they return to their own place, the fiery land of Bism, that they are happy again.

We here get a view of Lewis's deeply pastoral instincts. He was raised in the suburbs of Belfast at a point, he says, where the country met the town, and he conceived there a deep affection for the peace and privacy of unsullied nature. We remember that St. Anne's is a country estate beyond the last spur of the railroad, while the NICE want to turn sleepy little Edgestow into a noisy chaotic city like Birmingham. The Calormene capital of Tashbaan in Book 5 is seen as the seat of a vast tyranny and corruption. In comparison, Cair Paravel, the Narnian capital, is more of a country estate than a thriving administrative and mercantile center. We notice also, in Book 6, that the first king of Narnia, a London cabby originally from the country, loses his city-bred aggressiveness and flatness of speech once he is in the healthful air of Narnia for a few minutes. Lewis is obviously a person for whom the joys of nature and of solitude ring truest.

The adventure underground, then, is structured on contrasting images of joy and sadness. The gnomes' sadness is played against the prince's laughter. Both are signs of the witch's domination. At the end, however, after the witch is killed, the gnomes jump gleefully into Bism, while Rilian, like his father, remembers his duty and starts with new-found soberness toward his home in Narnia.

This pattern is repeated in the subsidiary action in which Jill, Eustace, and Aslan rout the bullies at school. The bullies are routed and the weak are gladdened. Yet we detect in the latter action a covert polemical intent not readily apparent in the former. The school is the embodiment of irreverent progressivism. It is called Experiment House; it is co-educational and secular and its evils result directly from the lack of traditional discipline. But we wonder why Lewis should want to lay these evils at the feet of educational innovation. Despite its secularism, despite the fact that it is a school for both boys and girls, we recognize behind his portrait the looming presence of Lewis's own public school. Despite its pretense to religiosity and reverence for tradition, Wyvern is the very model for the evils he criticizes in Experiment House. This, of course, is from the man who in *The Abolition of Man* had thrown down the gauntlet not just to positivism or secularism but to "the Innovator" (*AM*, 36) himself. Lewis's insecurity is getting in the way of a faithful and truthful rendering of modern society. The place is worse than it has to be and the joy of chastising the bullies a little too pure. "With the stength of Aslan in them, Jill plied her crop on the girls and Caspian and Eustace plied the flats of their swords on the boys so well that in two minutes all the bullies were running like mad, crying out, 'Murder! Fascists! Lion! It isn't *fair*'" (*SC*, 215).

Fortunately, it's not quite the bloodbath at Belbury but it's close enough. W.H. Lewis remarks that his brother was probably too harsh on his public school and suggests that he found so much evil precisely because he was looking for it (*L*, 4-5). We might suppose that his distaste for it was to some extent the cause and not the result of his bad treatment there, and that a young boy with Lewis's habits of privacy would not mix well to begin with. Lewis, who emphatically distinguishes his own fantasy from more typical children's fare, the "school story" in particular, because he feels that such stories pander to a child's basest desires for social eminence and constitute the rankest wish fulfillment, might have taken his own advice. An impulse, very strong, very narrow, and very evil, is coursing through this whole episode. Not only for the reader, but for the author as well, does this story constitute a sorry form of self-indulgence.

The fifth book of the series, *The Horse and His Boy*, is the story of Shasta, a boy living in Calormen, who is in reality the kidnapped son of the king of Archenland, Narnia's good neighbor. He leaves his home rather than be sold to a cruel Calormene noble, and flees to freedom in Narnia with the nobleman's horse, a free Talking Beast of Narnia, who has been a dumb slave for many years. On the way they join up with a girl of the Calormene nobility who is fleeing north rather than enter into an arranged marriage. They have many narrow escapes and while in Tashbaan, the capital, they learn of a plot by the Emperor's son Rabadash to conquer Archenland and from there to invade Narnia. Rushing across the desert, Shasta warns the king of Archenland and gathers reinforcements for the king in Narnia. The Calormenes are all killed or captured. Aslan changes Rabadash into a donkey and threatens that if he ever sets foot out of Tashbaan again he will change into a donkey forever. Consequently his reign is peaceful; he can't go to war himself and he can't send his generals off to win glory in war and return to overthrow him (his own father's route to power). Shasta is recognized as the king's lost son and raised as the heir apparent to the throne. Eventually he marries the girl.

The central virtue of the book is humility, which is carefully discriminated from its defect, pride, and its excess, that false humility which keeps one from daring all he should. On the political level this virtue is associated with the orderly reign of the High King Peter and contrasted with the autocracy of Calormen.

At first this seems like a complete break from the previous pattern where English children are brought to Narnia to be strengthened in virtue. About halfway through the book we meet Susan and Tumnus and much later on Lucy and Edmund, but this time they are adults, the kings and queens of the Golden Age, as well as very minor characters. But this may very well be a needed break. The first time reading the series one has the feeling that the pattern is getting a little too stiff: first the Pevensies; then when Peter and Susan get too old, Eustace; then when Lucy and Edmund get too old, Jill Pole. The progression in these earlier stories, moreover, is strictly forward in time; this one goes back to the time when the adventures first began and forces us to recover all the ground we have covered already.

Yet in a more basic sense the pattern is not broken at all. The four major characters, Shasta, the girl Aravis, and the two horses Bree and Hwim, act much like the Pevensies. The relationship starts out unbalanced, the noblewoman Aravis lording it over the humble fisher's lad, Shasta, the noble warhorse trying to think for demure Hwin. As the story progresses and Shasta shows great bravery and perseverance, Aravis comes to respect him more and herself less; Bree is chastised by Aslan, and Hwin, who had been closest to a normative character, shows forth in the eyes of the others with her true dignity. Similar also to earlier stories is Aslan's constant intervention on behalf of the travelers.

Moreover, *The Horse and His Boy* gives Lewis a chance to reiterate the importance of story in bringing souls to Christianity and in inculcating proper social virtues. For the novel is merely the retelling of a story popular at the court of Caspian. Like the New Testament in our own culture, *The Horse and His Boy* is important in keeping alive in latter-day Narnia the ideal of humility and the love of freedom. In fact, with the mention of the story fresh in our memory from *The Silver Chair*, it is almost like being at Caspian's court, sitting at a feast and listening to the bard calling to mind the virtues and heroism of the Golden Age. The importance of a cultural tradition for Lewis cannot be stressed too often.

The telling of a story is almost a good in itself. (The inability of the chief Duffer, in *Voyage of the Dawn Treader*, for instance, to tell his story well is just one more sign of his people's general culture and moral decadence.) Almost the only thing Lewis sees to admire in Calormen is its tradition of storytelling. We get a bit of the grand manner when Bree asks Aravis to tell them her story. That story is full of images, such as "the sun appeared dark in her eyes," and phrases, "Now it came to pass," that mark out a highly developed tradition of oral storytelling. The language is elevated and artificial, as when Aravis relates how Hwin kept her from suicide by saying, "'O my mistress, do not by any means destroy yourself, for if you live you may yet have good fortune but all the dead are dead alike.'" But Hwin remarks, "I didn't say it half so well as that" (*HB*, 35). It is very artificial but very effective:

> Aravis immediately began, sitting quite still and using a rather different tone and style from her usual one. For in Calormen, storytelling (whether the stories are true or made up) is a thing you're taught, just as English boys and girls are taught essay-writing. The difference is that people want to hear the stories, whereas I never heard of anyone who wanted to read the essays. (*HB*, 32)

This is not realism but it is perfectly in keeping with Lewis's own notions about stories. Stories are not there simply to be taken literally. In fact, he doesn't believe that there is a child alive stupid enough to believe in the wonders and marvels of his fairy tales. It is quite enough that a sense of wonder be stirred and the desire for "joy" be kindled.

Another important aspect of *The Horse and His Boy* is the way it extends the geographical boundaries of the world around Narnia. *The Voyage of the Dawn Treader* and *The Silver Chair* had both done this to a limited extent. But it is even more important in Book 5 because the book fulfills recurring hints about that other kingdom, Calormen, which also inhabits Narnia's world. Here in the south we find a dry treeless land whose basic feature is the glare of sun on sand. Matching the forbidding terrain is the character of the people and their works. Where Narnians are carefree and laughing, Calormenes are grave and mysterious; where one is open-handed, the other is "practical," tight-fisted, and miserly; where one is kind and gentle, the other is cruel and harsh.

We should probably, at this point, notice the British prejudice, which Lewis shares, against "wogs." But we should also recognize that Lewis makes a very un-British use of the stereotype. For Narnia is not Britain (but a fantasy refuge from Britain); it is a small, vulnerable country threatened with destruction by a large, warlike neighbor. The situation is much more like that of Greece and Persia, than Britain and Egypt (or India). In fact, we might even see in Calormen some of the evils which Lewis recognizes in Britain and in the modern world in general.

Tashbaan itself is a place of squalor, bad smells, and poverty-stricken crowds.

> It was much more crowded than Shasta had expected: crowded partly by the peasants (on their way to market) who had come in with them, but also with water-sellers, sweetmeat sellers, porters, soldiers, beggars, ragged children, hens, stray dogs, and barefooted slaves. What you would chiefly have noticed if you had been there was the smells, which came from unwashed people, unwashed dogs, scent, garlic, onions, and the piles of refuse which lay everywhere. (*HB*, 52)

It is a place rife with the evils of class distinctions. There is only one traffic regulation in Tashbaan: "Everyone who is less important has to get out of the way for everyone who is more important; unless you want a cut from a whip or a punch from the butt end of a spear" (*HB*, 53). The scene where the powerful Grand Vizier, Aravis's intended, grovels like a dog before the Tisroc, the emperor, and sustains the kicks of the emperor's son is equally telling. The worst of it is that no one sees how bad it is. Having just seen from concealment the Vizier's miserable treatment, Lasaraleen, a flighty acquaintance of Aravis who is hiding her from her father, tries to persuade her to stay and marry the man. "Won't you change your mind? Now that you've seen what a great man

Ahoshta is !" But Aravis is incensed. It takes a country girl like her to see through the pretenses of the great capital.

All in all, *The Horse and His Boy* is a very accomplished and workmanlike production from a writer who was feeling quite sure about what he wanted to say and how he wanted to say it. All the threads of the story fit quite nicely into the whole scheme. If there is not much of the magic that distinguishes earlier and later volumes in the series, it is not missed very much. The one bit of magic, the hermit's pool in which the final battle pitting Archenland and Narnia against the horde of Rabadash is viewed by Aravis and the horses, is mainly a bit of storytelling magic, i.e., it demonstrates the value of objective narraration by an omnipresent observer over the subjective viewpoint of large events.

The Magician's Nephew, the next volume, is magical with a vengeance. We can appreciate Lewis's canniness in sticking to a straight adventure for the preceding book. If he had continued to simply feed us one magical tale after another, we would have probably become bored with the device. Coming as it does on the heels of an adventure completely without magic, this story of magic rings, strange places, and evil magicians, is exceedingly marvelous and delightful.

Within the scheme of the whole sequence, this particular novel has two important functions. First of all it extends our knowledge of Narnia back to its very beginning and prepares us for the sudden eruption of evil into this benign world which we experience in Book 1. Moreover, it returns us to the centrality of the company of Narnia. Here we learn of its foundation. *The Magician's Nephew* is the story of how two Victorian children, Digory Kirke (Professor Kirke of *The Lion, the Witch, and the Wardrobe*) and Polly Plummer are the occasion for bringing evil into Narnia on the very morn of its birth. Digory's uncle, a dabbler in the black arts and a thoroughly nasty man, induces Polly to put a strange shimmering yellow ring on her finger, whereupon she immediately disappears. He then explains to Digory that he must go search for her and give her a green ring so she can return. The children however are only guinea pigs. Uncle Andrew is not at all sure that the green rings will work. Digory finds Polly in an enchanted wood full of pools that lead to different worlds, and after making sure they can return to London, they decide to explore the various worlds their rings give them access to. They discover first the dead world of Charn where Digory, against Polly's wishes, awakens an evil queen. They are forced to take her back to London. She threatens to destroy earth but the children succeed in getting her back to the wood and into another world. This world is Narnia at the moment of its creation. After some of the beasts are given the power of speech, a London cabby, who had, with his horse, been drawn along by the magic of the rings into Narnia, is made the first king of Narnia. Digory and Polly are sent for a seed which keeps the witch away from Narnia for many years, and Digory is rewarded with an apple which will heal his sick mother. The promise is made that even though the witch will rule over Narnia for a hundred years of winter, the sons of Adam and the daughters of Eve will eventually crush her. Digory plants the seed from the magic apple in his backyard. It grows into a tree which is toppled in a storm. From the wood is made the wardrobe through which the Pevensies first entered Narnia.

This is a development of the moral world we have experienced already in *The Silver Chair*. The unifying theme of the novel is not an action but an intellectually complex moral contrast, and the central moral act is considerably more complex too, involving as it does the choice of a spiritual good instead of a physical good. In *The Magician's Nephew*, the desolation caused by lust for power, represented in Charn, is contrasted with the fecund world created by Aslan. With *The Magician's Nephew*, the Narnia chronicles can be said to have reached a new stage of intellectual maturity. The crux of Digory's problem is whether he will take the fruit of the tree in the garden back to Aslan as he was instructed or home to his mother, who is dying and whom the fruit can cure. He must choose between two goods and not simply good and evil. The only clues he has to help him in this decision are the character of Aslan and the world he has created and the character of the witch, her world, and her would-be lover, Digory's fatuous Uncle Andrew.

Uncle Andrew exemplifies that priggery which Lewis sees as the chief danger of the intellectual life. He is a comic version of those same attitudes which Lewis had earlier dealt with in the figure of Weston. When Digory objects to his telling lies and endangering Polly's life, he replies:

> But of course you must understand that rules of that sort, however excellent they may be for little boys—and servants—and women—and even people in general, can't possibly be expected to apply to profound students and great thinkers and sages. No, Digory. Men like me possess hidden wisdom, are freed from common rules just as we are cut off from common pleasures. Ours, my boy, is a high and lonely destiny.... You will keep looking at everything from the wrong point of view.... Can't you understand that the thing is a great experiment? The whole point of sending anyone into the Other Place is that I want to find out what it's like.(*MN*, 18–22)

But of course he is too cowardly to go himself. "It's like asking a general to fight as a common soldier," is how he puts it. But he is only a pantomine demon.

The Queen of Charn is the real bill of goods. The witch represents the ultimate in human depravity and selfishness. She has destroyed her whole planet, peoples, cities, animals, and forests rather than lose her rule to her sister. The power of Lewis's portrait of her rests in his combination of imaginative materials ready at hand. The first of these is the decaying universe of H. G. Wells:

The wind that blew in their faces was cold, yet somehow stale. They were looking from a high terrace and there was a great landscape spread out below them. Low down and near the horizon a great, red sun, far bigger than our sun. Digory felt at once that it was also older than ours: a sun near the end of its life, weary of looking down upon that world. To the left of the sun, and higher up, there was a single star, big and bright. Those were the only two things to be seen in the dark sky; they made a dismal group. And on the earth, in every direction, as far as the eye could reach, there spread a vast city in which there was no living thing to be seen. And all the temples, towers, palaces, pyramids and bridges cast long, disastrous-looking shadows in the light of that withered sun. Once a great river had flowed through the city, but the water had long since vanished, and it was now only a wide ditch of grey dust. (*MN*, 59)

As we have already seen, the city is one of Lewis's favorite images for spiritual desolation, but the stale wind and giant red sun are images borrowed directly from Wells. Nonetheless they are effective and fresh because they are given a new and illuminating context. This is the personality of the queen herself. She is, as Digory recalls, the most beautiful woman he has ever seen. She has extraordinary physical and mental powers. She is unimaginably old. Digory finds her asleep with the corpses of her ancestors and we see her plan to establish her rule over London. Finally, she offers Digory and his mother everlasting life. Now if we feel that we've seen this all somewhere before, it's because we have. In fact, all these details belong to the central character of H. Rider Haggard's famous adventure, *She*. As with Haggard, Lewis's witch represents a consumate development of human personality, but a development which has the most evil consequences for it is selfish.

Contrasted with this dead world, we have Narnia where we see

a stretch of grassy land bubbling like water in a pot.... In all directions it was swelling into humps. They were of very different sizes, some no bigger than mole-hills, some as big as wheel-barrows, two the size of cottages. And the humps moved and swelled till they burst, and the crumbled earth poured out of them, and from each hump there came out an animal... the greatest moment of all was when the biggest hump broke like a small earthquake and out came the sloping back, the large, wise head, and the four baggy trousered legs of an Elephant. And now you could hardly hear the song of the Lion; there was so much cawing, cooing, crowing, braying, neighing, baying, barking, lowing, bleating, and trumpeting.(*MN*, 113–14)

Here we have the wonder of the creator (Lewis this time, as well as God) and his creation and that different relation of mind and matter spoken of in *That Hideous Strength*. It is a world full of growing things. Even the iron bar which the witch had thrown at the lion starts to grow into a lamppost. This gives Uncle Andrew ideas for a great industrial empire. "The commercial possibilities of this country are unbounded. Bring a few old bits of strab iron here, bury 'em, and up they come as brand new railway engines, battleships, anything you please. They'll cost nothing, and I can sell 'em at full prices in England. I shall be a millionaire" (*MN*, 111). But it gives Digory food for thought, so that when he encounters the witch and she tempts him to eat the fruit himself or else give it to his mother, he can resist. That the character of the witch at the moment of her ultimate defiance is particularly repulsive only helps to stiffen his resolve. "She was just throwing away the core of an apple which she had eaten. The juice was darker than you would expect and had made a horrid stain round her mouth. Digory guessed at once that she must have climbed in over the wall. And he began to see that there might be some sense in that last line about getting your heart's desire and getting despair along with it. For the witch looked stronger and prouder than ever, and even, in a way, triumphant: but her face was deadly white, white as salt" (*MN*, 159–60). All the metaphors of eating heretofore had been only trial runs for this fine passage.

It is interesting to note the intimate relation this novel has with Lewis's own biography. Professor Kirke could easily be Lewis himself, especially as he views his role as a Christian intellectual writing for children. As a child, Digory grows up at about the same time as Lewis. Like Lewis, he hates the city. And like Lewis, his mother is slowly dying. Like Lewis, Digory is tempted toward isolation and defiance, but he is able to see their true character even as Lewis is able to write a novel which mocks Uncle Andrew and underlines the profound evil represented by the witch.

Despite the book's general consistency of tone and incident, it does have small problems. As usual in the Narnia books, these problems are associated with the appearance of Aslan. Sometimes Lewis can't resist the opportunity to point to a moral, even though it doesn't happen to be the one his story makes— in this case about self-sacrifice. Aslan warns that the destruction on Charn is a pressing possibility for man in the 1950s. He tells Polly, "It is not certain that some wicked one of your race will not find out a secret as evil as the Deplorable Word and use it to destroy all living things. And soon, very soon, before you are an old man and an old woman, great nations in your world will be ruled by tyrants who care no more for joy and justice and mercy than the Empress Jadis" (*MN*, 178). Tyranny and atomic destruction are twin perils of the modern age. What is more interesting about this passage, however, is its tone of fatalism and political despair.

Although *The Magician's Nephew* ends on a note of conciliation and peace, this warning, which is seemingly adventitious, signals an important development in the plot and tone of the final book. Tyrants will rise, he says, and so Calormen, always jealous of the freedom of Narnia, makes another and successful attempt to subdue her neighbor. The door to the conquest is opened by Shift, an ape, who persuades his friend, the donkey, Puzzle, to wear a lion skin and parade himself as Aslan. As in the *Book of Revelations*, where the

Antichrist is a sign of troubles and apocalyptic change, the arrival of this Anti-Aslan marks the beginning of a period of great evil for Narnia and the approach of its final moments. Shift, speaking for the Anti-Aslan, orders the Talking Beasts to work in the Tisroc's mines and to cut down the Living Trees. King Tirian, learning of these things, despairs. He fears that the good and kind Aslan he had worshipped is actually cruel and demanding. In his despair he rashly kills two Calormenes who are beating a Talking Horse. But quickly he repents his evil action and with equal rashness surrenders himself to the false Aslan to be punished. As soon as he sees Puzzle, however, he realizes the hoax. Before he can alarm the other creatures, he is bound and gagged. At this point, he prays to the real Aslan for help. The two youngest of the company of Narnia, Jill and Eustace, appear to help him. But the cause is lost. The Calormenes have taken Cair Paravel. Formerly dependable members of Old Narnia, such as the dwarfs, have deserted not only the king but Aslan as well. The worst happens when the Calormene god, Tash (Satan himself), enters Narnia to take Puzzle's place. Eventually, Tirian, Jill, Eustace, and their friends, are captured and thrown into the stable, where Tash abides, as offerings to be devoured by him. But when they all enter the stable, they discover in it a green and sunlit country. Aslan greets them and banishes the evil Tash. The two children surprisingly meet the rest of the company of Narnia, Dr. Kirke and Polly and the four Pevenies. Then begins a mad race to "the garden in the West," which reveals itself to be another bigger and better Narnia. There they meet old friends—Caspian, Rilian, Reepicheep, and the rest—whom they had thought dead. The older children ask why they have been allowed to return to Narnia. Aslan tells them that this is not the same Narnia they had first entered; it is the "real Narnia" that the other had only been pointing to. They have all been killed in a train crash and can now receive their reward. And so began "the real story."

The central organizing principle of this story is once again a contrast, this time between the historical Narnia and the "real" Narnia. The organizing virtue, however, is more militant than the corresponding virtue in earlier books. It is the courage to face a desperate situation well. Not as intellectually complex as the preceding book, it is much more strenuous. There are, for instance, repeated comments critical of the Narnians for forgetting how to defend their country and their belief in Aslan. This helps set in perspective the hopeless lament of King Tirian, who wishes that he had died before all this talk of a cruel Aslan had begun. It also provides the angle from which to criticize the false humility of Puzzle, who lets the ape lead him into actions he knows are wrong.

The striking thing about this particular volume in the series is its bleakness of tone. This is partly the result of the use of a more objective narrative technique. Even in Book 6, intellectually the most complex of the series, the narrator is always making his presence felt in order to let us know that things are going to turn out all right. In *The Last Battle*, however, he is almost totally absent, especially at the beginning. This tone is also the product of the characters' hopelessness in the face of an awful situation. The parallels with *Revelations* also intensify the portents of disaster. But most of all it is involved with Lewis's evocation of another famous fantasy novel, George Orwell's *Animal Farm*. It is a thoroughly nasty and brutish world we enter as we open the pages of *The Last Battle*. Puzzle is unmercifully exploited by Shift and thinks no worse of Shift or himself for it. Like Orwell's pigs, Shift takes to wearing human clothes and to calling himself a man. He even strikes up a pact with humans, the Calormenes, to exploit the other animals. But this isn't an historical parable about the failure of the Communist Party. It is about the inability of a moral project like Narnia to survive in a world of economic exploitation and power politics. Shift and Puzzle have curiously abstract names, corresponding to a general human condition which their relationship is supposed to epitomize. The only way this condition can be overcome is to leave Narnia, which is ultimately subject to the same pressures as Earth, for the "real" Narnia, the land of heart's desire, where permanence and stability are guaranteed by Aslan.

Narnia is a decaying society in Book 7. The animals and humans are not prepared to defend it. The black dwarfs are as hostile to the king as they are to the Calormenes.

Lewis reveals his debt to Orwell in another way. The much reiterated slogan of the conspirators, "Tash is Aslan; Aslan is Tash," reminds us of double think, as well as of Orwell's—and Lewis's—horror of the abuse of language. This is, of course, also a continuation of Lewis's concern with distinguishing Christianity from other systems which attempt to swallow it up, e.g., Westonism and various other humanisms.

Some of the lightness and magic of the earlier books is recovered as soon as Tirian exchanges hope for despair. Yet it is a particularly cheerless adventure. The centaur, who is sent for reinforcements, is shot to death. The palace is captured. The dwarfs turn against Aslan and then the king. They indiscriminately murder Tirian's vassals and the Calormenes. It is only after the company enters the door of the stable that the tone of the novel changes significantly. Suddenly it is radiant and peaceful. For once they enter the door they are in the green sunlit plains of Aslan's kingdom. There they meet the rest of the company as well as the brave young Calormene whom Aslan had claimed for his own. From there they witness the awesome spectacle of the planet's death, a spectacle which adds extra poignance and savor to their own joyful situation. They speed across the landscape, swimming up waterfalls, scaling sheer mountains effortlessly, until they come at last to the real Narnia. They discover that time is merely the dream of eternity and observe that "the reason why we love the old Narnia is that it sometimes looked a little like this."

They learn that the spiritual is inconceivably more beautiful and wonderful than the material. "The further up and the further in you go, the bigger everything gets. The inside is larger than the outside" (*LB*, 180). This is the ultimate triumph of the subjective over the objective. Nothing good is ever lost. "But you are now looking at the England within England, the real England just as this is the real Narnia. And in that inner England no good thing is destroyed" (*LB*, 181).

The only element to disturb this harmony, the only trace of the sardonic and the bitter in this radiant universe is the fate of the black dwarfs who are thrown into the stable with Tirian and the children. They are blinded to the beauty around them; they see only darkness and smell only dung. Aslan offers them a glorious feast, but vulgar boors that they are, they horribly mistreat it.

> One said he was trying to eat hay and another said he had got a bit of old turnip and a third said he'd found a raw cabbage leaf. And they raised golden goblets of rich red wine to their lips and said "Ugh! Fancy drinking dirty water out of a trough that a donkey's been at! Never thought we'd come to this." But very soon every Dwarf began suspecting that every other Dwarf had found something nicer than he had, and they started grabbing and snatching, and went on to quarreling, till in a few minutes there was a free fight and all the good food was smeared on the faces and clothes or trodden under foot. (*LB*, 147)

As Walter Hooper says in his introduction to Lewis's essays on fairy tales and science fiction, Lewis detests politics, but we can't conclude from this that he refrains from criticizing various political groups or tendencies. His linking of the city and commerce with death and decay also has political overtones of an anarchistic nature. What we have, then, in the incident of the black dwarfs is a highly critical picture of the self-conscious working class. "The Dwarfs are for the Dwarfs" is obviously a parody of the Marxist maxim of "the working class for itself." But in this way, however, it seems much more selfish than it does in the Marxist context, where the working class constitutes the vast majority of the population as well as represents the noblest aspirations of the human race. But Marxists see that these aspirations are necessarily in conflict with the established order, while Lewis maintains that all anyone can do is fill his station in life.

This does not mean that Lewis is a "reactionary" so much as that his real interest is in another world, where there is real freedom and an escape from the world of government and economics he so abhors. We see this most clearly in *The Last Battle*. Faced with the imminent threat of tyranny and the ultimate defeat imposed by the end of the physical universe, human aspiration is driven "inward," a very revealing word, to the land of heart's desire. Thus Lewis's striving against his own subjectivistic tendencies never take him beyond his own subjective moral life and his personal circle of friendships. We again find that the real England is constituted, like the Logres, by "a happy few." Only in such a group does Lewis discover a happy accord between individuality and community which he sought all his life.

Lewis's last novel, *Till We Have Faces*, is a retelling of the Cupid and Psyche myth. Published the year after *The Last Battle*, it employs much the same brooding tone. But it also marks a return to the psychological interest of the science fiction trilogy. It traces the growth of ethical awareness in its narrator, Orual. As in his trilogy, Lewis is once again concerned with the tension between self-assertion and self-denial, between pride and love. Orual embodies Lewis's own problem—will she be "her own woman" or will she admit her responsibilities to other people and to the gods. In the course of her development she realizes that her life of political activity as a queen has been meaningless and has distracted her from her ethical duties to others. On the whole, it is a much more complex and powerful work than Lewis has ever written before. Owen Barfield calls it "the most muscular product of his imagination."

Orual, the oldest daughter of a petty king on the border of the Hellenistic world, tells the story of her youngest sister, Istra, whom their Greek tutor calls Psyche, of how Psyche is separated from her adoring older sister, and how they are brought together again. When Orual's mother dies, the king, who has already had two daughters by his first wife and is desperate for a male heir, takes another wife who dies giving birth to another girl. The father ignores her, but the child, under the loving care of Orual and "the Fox," the tutor, grows into a prodigy of beauty. She is so beautiful, in fact, that the people worship her as a goddess. But plague and drought are on the land and the priest of Ungit (the barbarian Aphrodite whose shape is a huge rock upon which the blood of countless sacrifices is spilled) says that the curse will be lifted only with the death of the accursed. The villain, says the priest, is Psyche, who parades herself as a goddess. She is taken to the mountain to be offered to the Beast, Ungit's son. Orual is too sick to go with the procession, but goes as soon as she is able in order to bury her sister's remains. She finds no body and after some searching finds her sister alive and thriving in a beautiful valley. Psyche tells her that "Westwind" swept her out of her bonds and brought her to the valley, to a beautiful palace, the home of a god, where gentle voices beckoned her enter, fed her, and bathed her. In the night the god came to her and made her his wife. He made her promise, however, that she would never look or ask to look at him. "But where is the palace," asks Orual. "Can you not see it," says Psyche, "We are sitting on its steps. Touch it." Orual, whose only thought has been to get Psyche away from the Mountain, thinks her mad and tries to wrestle her into submission but fails. Orual recrosses the river and spends the night with her guide, the captain of the palace guard, Bardia. During the night she sees a splendid castle but in a second it is gone. Convinced that the gods are only playing tricks with her, she resolves that she will tear Psyche from her madness even if she has to kill Psyche or herself. When she returns to the mountain, she again tries to persuade Psyche to leave or else to look at the god, but her sister remains firm. Finally Orual stabs herself in the arm and threatens to do worse not only to herself but to Psyche as well. Knowing how dire the consequences of her disobedience will be, Psyche nevertheless agrees to look at the god. That night Orual watches from across the river as Psyche uncovers the lamp. The next moment a great voice rends the night, a storm rages, and the god appears to Orual, looks upon her with great disdain, and prophesies that "You also shall be Psyche." Orual hears her weeping sister moving away down the valley but is unable to reach her in the storm. In the morning the beautiful valley is a desolate wasteland. Orual returns home thwarted in her plans to regain her sister, and sets about burying the pain of her love by diligent application to swordcraft and affairs of state. The rest of part 1 recounts her successes as queen. Through it all, however, she apprehensively waits for the punishment meted out to her sister to overtake her. In the final pages of the section she recounts how she came to write the book. She discovered a temple to Psyche in which the story of the goddess—told by an ignorant old priest—tells how her trials resulted from the jealousy and treachery of her sisters. Orual accuses the gods of lying and of taking from her the only thing she ever loved.

Part 2, much shorter, involves a recantation of the original draft and an admission that most of it was distortion and lies. The first chink in the armour of her self-righteousness is caused by her meeting with the eunuch Tiran who had once very long before been her sister Redival's lover. He tells her how Redival, whom Orual had always despised as shallow and flighty, was so lonely when Orual abandoned her first for the Fox and then for Psyche that she threw herself at every man who came along. The second is when Orual learns how much she has used and used up her subordinates. Bardia's wife tells her that she is "gorged with other men's lives; women's too. Bardia's, mine, the Fox's; your sister's; both your sisters'" (*TWHF*, 275). Then come her dreams and visions. First she dreams that she is Ungit devouring all that comes within her power. She tries to kill herself, but the god, who had appeared to her earlier, tells her she cannot escape Ungit by going to the land of the dead. She resolves to practice true philosophy, as her tutor had instructed her, but she finds herself lapsing into the same evils. She dreams that she is trampled by a herd of golden sheep, which she interprets in her despair as a sign that the divine wrath can in no way be swayed from exacting its toll of her. Another dream comes in which she is Ungit's slave and must dip her bowl in the river Styx. But when an eagle asks her what she wants, the bowl has changed into her book. She is borne suddenly underground by shadow people to a great chamber where she is instructed to read her complaint. But where before she had seen only justice and righteousness, she now sees her own selfishness echoed in every word. The shade of her tutor then leads her to a room in which the trials of Psyche are figured in murals on the walls. But the tasks that Orual had despaired of in her dreams, Psyche accomplished with lightness of heart and relative ease. Finally she meets the goddess Psyche has become, more beautiful but more like herself than ever before. But Orual has learned her lesson. She admits her selfishness. "Never again will I call you mine." And then the god comes, dreadful and beautiful, with the fulfillment of the prophecy. It is not the dread punishment she had expected for so long, but a gift of beauty. The manuscript breaks off shortly after this, at a point where Orual renounces her hatred and denunciation of the gods. In the postscript, Arnom, the new priest of Ungit and counsellor to Orual, asks that the manuscript be taken to Greece.

From this outline we can see that Lewis retains all the major features of the action of the myth as told by Apuleius: the goddess' wrath, the sacrifice, the love of Cupid for Psyche, the treachery of her sister and her trials. But the changes are even more significant. Cupid is no skulking adolescent who has a go-between instruct that the girl be sacrificed. Instead the charge comes directly from the priest of the goddess. The king is a much more unsavory character, a lecher, a drunkard, and a tyrant to his daughters. Psyche, on the other hand, is a much severer and loftier character than in the Latin novel. She disobeys her lord not by imbibing the fears of her sister; she is true to him and disobeys only lest her sister do further violence to herself. In the final trial, moreover, when she is sent on a journey to the Queen of the Dead to ask for beauty for her mistress Ungit, she is admonished to speak to no one, and she withstands the pleas not only of a shadow-Fox but also a mock-Orual to address them. In Apuleius, she not only receives no such injunction, but falls victim to her own pride and curiosity by opening the box to take some of the beauty for herself. Lewis's Psyche, finally, fulfills her tasks with a grave joy not hinted at by Apuleius.

The temptation, also, is much different. In *The Golden Ass*, Psyche's sisters, both beautiful and themselves married to kings, see her splendid home and envy her good fortune. They are simply jealous and wish to ruin her happiness. In Lewis's version, there is only one tempter and she is very ugly and unmarried. She ruins Psyche's idyll not out of envy, she says, but out of love and a desire for her sister's happiness. This is only to point, however, to the major difference between the two works and that is the difference in points of view. Apuleius' version is basically that given by the old priest at the shrine of Psyche. Good persons and evil persons are easily sorted out and all motives are patently clear. This is precisely what Orual is reacting against. What makes the story so interesting is that it is told from an antagonistic point of view. This is the first time Lewis has given a warped consciousness full control of one of his books, and the tension between the story as Orual imagines it and the real story produces art of a very high order. We must not confuse this technique with that used in *Screwtape*. There we could not mistake Screwtape's words for the truth;

here we can almost believe Orual. Further complicating the effect is the fact that there is no simple dichotomy between belief and unbelief. At least at first, the alternative between belief in the bloody primordial earth-goddess Ungit and the shallow but sincere rationalism of the Greek tutor is not heavily weighted on the side of belief.

Moreover, the structure of the book is highly complex, consisting of a series of contrasts on different but complementary levels. On the cultural and economic level we have a contrast between the kingdom as it existed under King Trom, Orual's father, and the reformed kingdom under Queen Orual. In the first stage agriculture and war are its only products; plague, drought, and famine are common; and a mirror from the Greek lands or a slave with a Greek education are signs of a paramount culture. In the second:

> I had all the laws revised and cut in stone in the centre of the city. I narrowed and deepened the Shennity till barges could come up to our gates. I made a bridge where the old ford had been. I made cisterns so that we should not go thirsty whenever there was a dry year. I became wise about stock and bought in good bulls and rams and bettered our breeds. (*TWHF*, 245)

Drought and famine are put at abeyance. Wars are averted by skillful diplomacy, and commerce is encouraged.

On the religious level, the old goddess is a rude stone said to have been pushed from the bowels of the earth. Her house is a dark narrow egg-shaped pile of stone filled with the stench of blood. She is a jealous goddess demanding the wastage of the best of the people's cattle as well as their most beautiful daughters. The new goddess, a piece of wood shaped by the hand of man, by an artist somewhat trained in the Greek technique, is housed in the old temple which has been newly brightened and which is freshly washed after each sacrifice. Yet for all its rudeness and barbarism, the old religion is much more heartfelt, much closer to real worship than the abstract and arcane mutterings of the new priest. An old woman explains her sacrifice to the old Ungit, saying, "Ungit has given me great comfort. There's no goddess like Ungit.... That other, the Greek Ungit, she wouldn't understand my speech. She's only for nobles and learned men. There's no comfort in her" (*TWHF*, 283). The old Ungit is also capable of uniting the dissident elements of the kingdom. Finally, unlike the new priest, who doesn't really believe in the old religion but uses it to achieve power, the old priest through his belief generates real authority. As Orual herself admits:

> The Fox had taught me to think—at any rate to speak—of the Priest as of a mere schemer and a politic man who put into the mouth of Ungit whatever might most increase his own power and lands or most harm his enemies. I saw it was not so. He was sure of Ungit. Looking at him as he sat with the dagger pricking him and his blind eyes unwinking, fixed on the King, and his face like an eagle's face, I was sure too. Our real enemy was not a mortal. The room was full of spirits, and the horror of holiness. (*TWHF*, 62)

As is suggested by this quote, this contrast is repeated on the intellectual level in the contrast between the Fox, who taught the new priest as well as the daughters of the king, and the old priest. The epitome of the fox's wisdom is involved in the Stoic acceptance of the evils of life. "Today I shall meet cruel men, cowards and liars, the envious and the drunken. They will be like that because they do not know what is good from what is bad. This is an evil which has fallen upon them and not upon me. They are to be pitied"...(*TWHF*, 76). But when he meets true belief as in the person of the priest he is reduced to mere sophistries and scoffing. He is a victim of his own logic-chopping. As Psyche, facing the day of sacrifice, says:

> The Priest has been with me. I never knew him before. He is not what the Fox thinks. Do you know, Sister, I have come to feel more and more that the Fox isn't the whole truth. Oh, he has much of it. It'd be dark as a dungeon within me but for his teaching. And yet...I can't say it properly. He calls the whole world a city. But what's a city built on? There's earth beneath. And outside the wall? Doesn't all the food come from there as well as all the dangers?...things growing and rotting, strengthening and poisoning, things shining wet...in one way (I don't know which way) more like, yes, even more like the House of [Ungit]. (*TWHF*, 78–79)

Orual is actually much more like the priest than like the fox in that she also believes passionately in the gods. Only she hates them. "It never entered the Fox's mind—he was too good to believe that the gods are real, and viler than the vilest man" (*TWHF*, 79). She is the believer manque and on the ethical level of the novel she is completely contrasted with Psyche, whose faith in the god is as deep as Orual's hate. As a relief from her failure with Psyche, Orual submerges herself in affairs of state. Yet this involves a kind of perversion and a kind of death. "I did and I did and I did—and what does it matter what I did." The mask that she wears throughout her reign is a sign of her alienation not only from her subjects but also from herself. The novel suggests that she becomes less a woman and more a man; the affective impulses, which are to Lewis woman's closest ties to nature, are stifled. It is an insight typical of Lewis. Her horrified distaste for the womblike oppressiveness of Ungit's house reminds us of Jane Studdock. Her reaction is comparable to Janes's horror at the unbaptized Venus.

Orual's love is no more than a kind of spiritual greed, thereby proving herself the direct descendant of Screwtape and the Mother in *The Great Divorce*.

> Orual is (not a symbol) but an instance, a "case" of human affection in its natural condition, true, tender, suffering, but in the long run tyrannically possessive and ready to turn to hatred when the beloved ceases to be its possession. What such love particularly cannot stand is to see the beloved passing into a sphere where it cannot follow. (*L*, 274)

At times her hate is directed as much at Psyche as at the god.

Psyche, on the other hand, does all she can to admit Orual to her happiness and then sacrifices her own happiness for her. Finally, however, her sacrifices make Orual realize the strength and unselfishness of true love. Psyche is, as Lewis calls her in one of his letters, *"anima naturaliter Christiana."*

> It was beauty that did not astonish you till afterwards when you had gone out of sight of her and reflected on it. While she was with you, you were not astonished. It seemed the most natural thing in the world. As the Fox delighted to say, she was "according to Nature;" what every woman, or even everything, ought to have been and meant to be, but had missed by some trip of chance. (*TWHF*, 30)

She is the epitome of glorified nature, "Nature" under divine direction and as such already almost a goddess. She embodies the obedience, faith, and loyalty, which Lewis desired in the education of Jane Studdock.

Yet if this contrast embodies ideas we have already seen about the nature of women and displays an attitude toward politics—that it is a distraction from the important issue of personal salvation—perfectly consonant with earlier writings, the relation of these two characters reveal on another level the spiritual autobiography of the author. We can see in Orual's ugliness some of Lewis's apprehension at his own physical unattractiveness, and in the king's choleric personality something of Lewis's father. Moreover, if we let Orual stand for Lewis's public self and Psyche for the real self capable of expressing "joy," we have just the major developments Lewis traces in his autobiography. From the unconscious and innocent love and enjoyment of one in the other during childhood, we come to Orual's attempt to win Psyche back from her other love, the love for whose sake she was so beautiful. This suggests Lewis's attempt to win the subjective experience for its own sake rather than seeking out "the object of his desire." We also have in both the two separate lives, the real self drawing one ever onward to a final confrontation with God, and the public self concerned with the bric-a-brac of social and political existence and with its own selfish demands and sense of worth. Finally, we have in both the confrontation with and adherence to the god.

It is easier to understand the richness of this novel if we have before us not only the framework of the myth but also the key developments of Lewis's own life. This core of biographical truth allows Lewis to develop his pairs of theses and antitheses with unusual assurance. All these levels revolve around the basic dilemma of Orual's choice, which is also Lewis's choice—will he give himself wholeheartedly to the god or will he reject him. Politics and rationalism, although important to a total picture of the world, are ways of avoiding the issue, and ultimately ways of fighting him. This is why the action of the novel becomes more and more interiorized—in dreams and visions—toward the end. We are approaching the arena of real importance.

It is a very fine novel. Lewis develops his ideas and characters with complexity and richness. An idea does not condemn a person in *Till We Have Faces*; the Fox is better than he says. His kindness and loving care for Orual speak of a deeper philosophy than he perhaps knows. Even the cultural and social setting seem well researched and well thought out, even despite the obvious parallel with the modern situation as well as Lewis's own ideological bias. The transition from a communal religion to a class religion is a particularly fine observation on the role of ideology in social revolutions. It is the kind of point Lewis in his other fantasies does not take care to attend to.

The only thing the novel does not really convince us of is the *total* worthlessness of Orual's political activity. She accomplishes real goods during her reign, whatever the character of her personal life. This incompatibility between story and theme reveals once again Lewis's own deep alienation from politics.

Lewis's productions after this are all extremely minor and can be described in a sentence or two. The story "Forms of Things Unknown" is about an astronaut who meets a gorgon on the moon and is turned to stone; it is meant to illustrate the observation in *Perelandra* "that what was myth in one world might always be fact in another" (*OOW*, 119). "Ministering Angels" is the closest, I think, Lewis ever gets to bedroom farce. A scientific study reveals that astronauts cannot go without sex for the long, long periods of space travel without becoming psychopathic. The only two women the government can get, however, to minister to their tensions are a fat aging madame and a thin-lipped, flat-chested spinster who believes in science and sexual therapy. Obviously, the astronauts do not take up the offer. "The Shoddy Lands" is slightly more interesting. It portrays Lewis's fall into the nightmare world of a modern woman's consciousness.

> Here and there in the shoddy grass there were patches of what looked, from a distance, like flowers. But each patch, when you came close to it, was as bad as the trees and the grass. You couldn't make out what species they were supposed to be. And they had no real stems or petals; they were mere blobs. As for the colors, I could do better myself with a shilling paintbox. (*OWW*, 101)

Eventually he comes upon a giant woman, better built and with better teeth than the real woman but obviously the same girl, admiring herself naked in a mirror. Nothing is real in this world except what contributes to her own monstrous egoism. We wouldn't do the author any disservice if we saw behind his diatribe his own failures with women. We might even accuse him of fashioning a woman worthy of his fear, a kind of self-congratulatory fantasy.

Lewis's final attempt at fantasy, an unfinished novel to be called *After Ten Years*, was another retelling of myth, this time the Trojan War. As in *Till We*

Have Faces, the interest is more on personal psychology, personal relations, and ethical decision than the panorama and sweep of war. The novel opens with the final battle at Troy and the question posed is, after the war what are this aging warrior and this aging beauty queen, Menelaus and Helen, to make of each other? For Menelaus the problem is more acute. Will he live with the real Helen or with his memory of her? The problem is not resolved, but it remains an interesting fragment if only for Lewis's ability to unite his various interests, the moral and the mythical, into a fiction which makes the legendary concrete and which gives the familiar an archetypal status.

If Lewis's primary attitudes can be said to have developed at all after his mythical novels, it would have to be in the direction of increasing despair over modern social and political life. After the calm and relative unconcern of early Narnia and *Till We Have Faces*, statements in his letters about the "frightening monotony" of modern life become quite common. The conscientious man finds himself increasingly frustrated and overwhelmed by the tyranny of modern institutions. In a letter to I.O. Evans, he says:

> There is a grain of seriousness in my sally against the Civil Service. I don't think you have worse taste or worse hearts than other men. But I do think the State is increasingly tyrannical and you, inevitably, are among the instruments of that tyranny. . . . This doesn't matter for you who did most of your service when the subject was still a free man. For the rising generation it will become a real problem at what point the policies you are ordered to carry out have become so iniquitous that a decent man must seek some other profession. (*L*, 259–60)

Capping this pessimism is an addition made to a 1962 edition of Screwtape entitled "Screwtape Proposes a Toast." On one level, it represents a return to the polemical stridency of some twenty years earlier. Worse than that, Lewis, for all his railing against it, once again reveals himself as a prig. Taken as a whole, the piece is a lament over the irremediable mediocrity of modern life.

> For "democracy" or the "democratic spirit" (diabolical sense) leads to a nation without great men, a nation mainly of sub-literates full of cocksureness which flattery breeds on ignorance, and quick to snarl or whimper at the first hint of criticism.(*SL*, 169)

The moral consequence of the great progressive ideas of the nineteenth century—freedom and equality—is a spread of the spiritual disease of envy, the feeling "which prompts a man to say *I'm as good as you*" (*SL*, 162). The only reaction to the tyranny of the "Normal" and "Regular" has been the alienation of the intelligentsia, which "is very useful to the cause of Hell" (*SL*, 164). Lewis's own position is not, of course, very different from the secular and atheist intellectuals he criticizes. It is a matter of attitude. He won't have any of the half-baked correctives of the Marxists or the behaviorists. He wants his fantasy of the good old England where "children have been made to work in school, where talent is placed in high posts, and where the ignorant mass are allowed no say at all in public affairs"(*SL*, 169). But even this attitude isn't any less alienated than the intellectuals he criticizes. He doesn't have a politic or even a consistent social ideal. Both his Christianity and his fantasy are ways of escaping the problems of modern society.

The most damning thing that can be said about Lewis's lack of politics is that he fails—on his own terms, as an ethical thinker—to deal with problems of property, status, and social organization, which absorb so much of the attention of the adult in bourgeois society. This has generally been recognized even by those sympathetic to Lewis. Chad Walsh says, "His blueprints for personal morality are clear and usable, but we have seen that he offers little guidance to the Christian concerned with the largescale application of religion to society."[1] Walsh concludes that Lewis did so much else well that it is wrong to criticize him for failing to deal with this one area. But is it? Lewis might more reasonably have been expected to avoid theorizing about sex. He was a bachelor, after all, till he was 58, and he displayed little or no interest in women before that time. Yet he devotes a great deal of time and energy, in *Perelandra* and *That Hideous Strength*, especially, to discussing the proper roles of the sexes. But this is not the case with politics. Except for scattered comments in which he is by turns an arch-conservative and an anarchist, he never in all his work seriously considers politics as a source of value. Lewis's attitude represents almost a complete bracketing of these concerns. Class and social position is always a matter of destiny—the three biologically distinct species of Mars pursue their different kinds of labor in complete harmony and satisfaction; the Pevensies become kings and queens of Narnia in fulfillment of a prophecy. This is strange because, given Lewis's penchant for alternative worlds, one would have thought that he had enough imaginative freedom to create an alternative social organization. But there is no rival organization—only a vague longing for freedom from worrying about such things.

From *Spirits in Bondage*, his first volume, to *Till We Have Faces*, his last completed novel, his heroes are confronted by the impoverishment of social and political life. As a result, the metaphor of flight and escape is a central one in his work. In *Spirits in Bondage*, he escapes "the scarlet city" for a "green Hidden Country." In *Dymer* the hero flees the authoritarian "Perfect City" for the forest. In *The Pilgrim's Regress*, John flees Puritania and its Landlord (God), who "was quite extraordinarily kind and good to his tenants, and would certainly torture most of them to death the moment he had the slightest pretext," for an island he had seen in a vision. In the science fiction trilogy, Ransom leaves war-ravaged England for the splendors of Venus. In *The Lion, the Witch, and the Wardrobe*, the Pevensies escape the boredom of their childish existence into the magical world of Narnia. It is no coincidence, either, that this story like the science fiction trilogy opens in time of war. In *The Last Battle*, at a time when Narnia has ceased to be benign and uncomplicated, when it succumbs to problems of politics and oppression, the imaginary world is destroyed, and the company retreats into "the real Narnia" where permanence and stability are guaranteed by God. In *Till We Have Faces*, Orual's political activity becomes meaningless to her and an escape, to reverse the image, from really important ethical concerns.

As we have seen, Lewis's unconcern with politics and his flight from political society into fantasy is a response to a situation in which all political and social realities assumed a threatening aspect. The first such reality, of course, was his father. After the death of his mother, but even before, his father, a well-to-do lawyer, was very remote and inaccessible to his sons. Lewis imitated his father's preoccupation with politics in his earliest stories as a child but this temporary enthusiasm failed to close the distance between father and son. Yet Lewis, for all his distrust of his father and what he stood for, still admired his father greatly. His ambivalence toward his father hardened into a pattern of withdrawl from politics and society only after his various disasters at school, especially his public school at Wyvern. Hereafter his interests were limited to imaginative literature and to a small circle of friends. So tough was this armor that even World War I failed to make much of a dent. It is this withdrawl from the competition, status-seeking, and materialism of bourgeois society—as experienced in the person of his father and later in his schools—which forms the basis of his various personal concerns, fantasy literature and Christianity being the two most prominent of them. But as we have seen, Christianity, with its guarantee of heaven, is a logical extension of the fantasy impulse. Thus if W.H.Auden is right in saying of Yeats that "mad Ireland hurt you into poetry," we might say with equal truth of Lewis that mad Ireland (and England) hurt him into fantasy.

5

J.R.R. Tolkien and His Critics

One of the more noteworthy phenomena of recent literary history has been the enormous popular success of J.R.R. Tolkien's fantasy trilogy, *The Lord of the Rings*. After ten years of underground notoriety, mostly in intellectual circles, it suddenly burst aboveground in 1965 with the publication of two separate paperback editions. Over 250,000 copies of the trilogy were sold the first year and sales have been brisk ever since. Moreover, as a result of the trilogy's success, paperback editions of *The Hobbit*, a children's story published in 1937 which serves as a prelude to the Ring, as well as a *Tolkien Reader*, were brought out. In fact, Tolkien became one of the few genuine crazes of the sixties, complete with buttons and T-shirts saying "Frodo Lives" and wallsized maps of his invented world, Middle-earth. One critic reported an enthusiast who had read the whole Ring thirty times with no sign of a let-up. Most of this success, of course, has been with a very young audience, and there have been any number of speculations as to the reasons for its success with this particular audience, but the probable reasons are quite apparent. The world of the Ring is based on the conflict of two diametrically opposed powers struggling for unrivaled supremacy. For those of us who have grown up with the ideology of the cold war, this strikes a very familiar note. But beyond this, Tolkien gives his story a happy ending—an absolute necessity, he remarked in 1938, for a fairy story. He gives his audience a "consolation" (his own term) which cannot be verified by historical experience but which for that very reason is all the more desired.

Now Tolkien categorically denies any parallel between his story and the contemporary world, but no author can guarantee what his readers will make of his work. His readers respond to his novel in an ideological context in which the conflict of two rival "ideologies" irreconcilably opposed to one another, one capitalistic, the other communist, one "democratic," the other "totalitarian," has become a fact of practical existence. Given the sense of powerlessness which many people feel in response to the complexities of modern social and economic life and given a world situation which threatens holocaust every six months, it is not difficult to see why the young have responded with uncommon enthusiasm to what Edmund Wilson has derisively called a "children's book which has somehow got out of hand." For, better than any other recent fantasist, Tolkien has evoked the sense of crisis, of impending devastation with which most of us must live.

Besides his tremendous success with the young, Tolkien has, with the notable exception of Edmund Wilson, achieved considerable critical success. Typical of the appreciative comments is this remark by Richard Hughes: "What can I say then? For *width* of imagination it almost beggars parallel, and it is nearly as remarkable for its vividness and for the narrative skill which carries the reader on, enthralled, for page after page."[1] But C.S. Lewis, Tolkien's good friend and fellow don, finds more in Tolkien's work than just artistic *esprit*. "If Ariosto rivalled it in invention (in fact, he does not) he would still lack its heroic seriousness."[2] In fact, quite a few critics have seen more in Tolkien's work than just a pleasant way to dispose of two weeks' leisure.

There have been numerous differences of opinion, of course, as to what Tolkien is saying in *The Lord of the Rings*. Most of the controversy has centered on the relationship between Tolkien's interest in Norse mythology and his avowed commitment to Christianity. Behind this controversy is the general sense that Norse myth, to which Tolkien is indebted for place names, situations, characters, and the general somberness of his work, is somehow in conflict with Christian mythology. Ragnarok, Gotterdammerung, the death of Baldur all embody the pessimistic Norse sense of history. The Christian sense of history, on the other hand, is fundamentally optimistic. Such concepts as the millenium and Providence express a confidence that history is being guided by divine goodness toward a happy ending.

Gunnar Urang, in his essay "Tolkien's Fantasy: the Phenomenology of Hope," emphasizes Tolkien's relationship to Christian dogma. He stresses the importance which Tolkien, in his writing on fairy stories, places on the happy ending. What Tolkien presents us with, he says, is not an overt reconstruction of Christian myth (as one gets, for example, with C.S. Lewis) but rather a sense of providential design; we see the history moving toward a happy and successful end. And, if the characters ever doubt or lose sight of that end, they are given providential warnings or signs which will put them back on the right track.

Perhaps the most extremely stated case on behalf of Tolkien's Norse influence is that of William Ready in his book *Understanding Tolkien:* "This is Tolkien's great contribution to the canon of supernatural literature, no more need there be even hope of a happy ending. The decision to struggle on when defeat seems inevitable is the true glory of Man that Tolkien has brought forward again from the great Norse ideal."[3] Ready, however, fails in his book to come to terms with Tolkien's declaration that a necessary part of his fiction is the happy ending, in which evil is destroyed, good rewarded, and the order of society restored. Tolkien makes this very clear in his comments on the function of consolation in fairy stories.

Almost I would venture to assert that all complete fairy-stories must have it. At least I would say that Tragedy is the true form of Drama, its highest function; but the opposite is true of Fairy-story. Since we do not appear to possess a word that expresses this opposite—I will call it *Eucatastrophe.* The *eucatastrophic* tale is the true form of fairy-tale, and its highest function. The consolation of fairy-stories, the joy of the happy ending: or more correctly of the good catastrophe, the sudden joyous "turn" for there is no true end to any fairy-tale: this joy, which is one of the things which fairy-stories produce supremely well, is not essentially "escapist," nor "fugitive"... It does not deny the existence of *dyscatastrophe,* of sorrow and failure: the possibility of these is necessary to the joy of deliverance: it denies (in the face of much evidence, if you will) universal final defeat and in so far is *evangelium,* giving a fleeting glimpse of Joy, Joy beyond the walls of the world, poignant as grief. (*TR,* 68)

C.S. Lewis was Tolkien's good friend and worked beside him at Oxford for many years. In his comment on *The Lord of the Rings,* he tried to establish a middle ground, explaining the compatibility of the Norse and Christian world views. In an essay, entitled "The Dethronement of Power," he says:

Every time we win we shall know that our victory is impermanent. If we insist on asking for the moral of the story, that is its moral: a recall from facile optimism and wailing pessimism alike, to that hard, yet not quite desperate, insight into Man's unchanging predicament by which heroic ages have lived. It is here that the Norse affinity is strongest. (*DP,* 15)

Like Ready, Lewis insists that the Norse influence is predominant. For Lewis, however, this does not exclude the possibility of Christian hope. Tolkien, he believes, is making a statement about the world of men, in which Sauron-like polities have ever and will always arise to threaten the peace and prosperity of their neighbors. One of the things Lewis finds most attractive about Tolkien's fantasy world is "surprisingly, its realism."

This war has the very quality of the war my generation knew. It is all here: the endless, unintelligible movement, the sinister quiet of the front when "everything is now ready," the flying civilians, the lively, vivid friendships, the background of something like despair and the merry foreground, and such heavensent windfalls as a cache of choice tobacco "salvaged" from a ruin. (*DP,* 14)

Tolkien's fiction, then, fits right into Lewis's own project of criticism and escape from the modern world. Like *The Last Battle* it provides evidence of the danger and desolation of political and social life and insists, in its own way, on an alternative reality which will serve as a refuge from chaos and suffering. We have noted in an earlier chapter how many of Lewis's imaginary voyages began in time of war. It is no coincidence that Tolkien's interest in fantasy was, as he tells us, "quickened to full life by war" (*TR,* 42).

John Ronald Reuel Tolkien was born in 1892 in Bloemfontein, in the central portion of the Union of South Africa. Although the name is of German ancestry, both Tolkien's parents were originally from Birmingham, an industrial center in the English Midlands. Tolkien's father, a bank manager, died when Tolkien was only four years old, and Tolkien's mother returned with her two sons to Birmingham. His experience of the industrial city was almost completely negative. One critic suggests that the wastes and deserts which define the evil realm of Mordor owe a great deal to the grim dark city of Tolkien's boyhood. For Tolkien the real England is the English countryside, the England of small farms, wide fields, and rolling pasture lands. It is this domesticated humanized landscape which is the basis for not only C.S. Lewis's Narnia but also for Tolkien's Shire. Although he was born in South Africa, Tolkien nevertheless felt it to be an alien landscape. When he finally arrived in England, at the age of three-and-a-half or four, he had the oddly paradoxical feeling that he was seeing something new and yet that he was coming home.[4] It is this feeling of both strangeness and hominess which pervades his conception of the Shire. In 1904, when Tolkien was twelve, his mother died, and he and his brother went to live with a Roman Catholic priest, Fr. Francis Xavier Morgan at the Birmingham Oratory.

Tolkien himself has not said much at all about this early period of his life. Beyond a recital of the basic facts, he has added only that "it was not an unhappy childhood. It was full of tragedies, but it didn't tot up to an unhappy childhood." One critic, Mr. William Ready, however, has felt impelled to elaborate on these basic facts. The Birmingham Oratory had been founded by John Henry, Cardinal Newman in an attempt to instill a measure of learning and respectability in the Roman Church in England. Yet the Church was to remain stigmatized by the fact that the vast majority of its members were simple, uneducated Irishmen drawn to England, as they were to the United States, by the promise of work and a better life. Given this milieu, suggests Ready, the priests and students of the Birmingham Oratory must have felt out of step not only with England but even with their own Church, and Tolkien himself "must have known through Father Morgan some of the dusty feeling of defeat that pervaded the place."[5]

It would be interesting to know how much of this is authentic and how much fictionalized. Ready goes on to connect the isolation and feeling of defeat, which he claims Tolkien experienced as a student at the Oratory, with the sense of impending doom which threatens Middle-earth and the profound isolation which surrounds the Ring-bearer, Frodo. Perhaps this is a little too ingenious. As Tolkien himself, says, "A real taste for fairy-stories was wakened by philology on the threshold of manhood, and quickened to full life by war." (*TR*, 42). Certainly we need not go any further than the dangers and profound personal losses Tolkien experienced in the war, in accounting for the anxiety and premonitions of disaster which haunt Tolkien's work.

After his schooling in Birmingham, Tolkien entered Oxford. In 1915 he joined the British army and served as an officer in the Lancashire Fusiliers from

1915 to 1918. Tolkien was uncommonly fortunate to have survived that long a time in the service, yet it was a good fortune which left a bitter taste in his mouth.

> One has indeed personally to come under the shadow of war to feel fully its oppression; but as the years go by it seems now often forgotten that to be caught in youth by 1914 was no less hideous an experience than to be involved in 1939 and the following years. By 1918 all but one of my close friends were dead. (*FR*, xi)

In the same paragraph Tolkien suggests that the "story-germ" for *The Lord of the Rings* is indeed this disastrous war experience.

In 1916 he married Miss Edith Bratt, who was later to become the mother of this three sons and one daughter. After Armistice, he returned to college and received his M.S. in 1919. Before beginning a career teaching, Tolkien worked for about two years on the Oxford English Dictionary.

He had been interested in invented languages since his youth, and in the period after the war, he began to develop a world, Middle-earth, in which these languages and the imaginary peoples who spoke them would have a home. In addition, he purposed to develop a mythology for England, comparable in its grandeur and scope to the Norse mythologies. Out of these stories and this purpose grew a work originally called "The Book of Lost Tales" and later titled *The Silmarilion*. He did not complete this work—so grand was his purpose that any attempt would necessarily prove inadequate—but he continued to polish and revise it from time to time until his death. In addition, it provided the background for the two most important of his later fantasies, *The Hobbit* and *The Lord of the Rings* trilogy.

In 1920 he took a position as Reader at the University of Leeds. His first important work of scholarship was published two years later, *A Middle-English Vocabulary*. In 1924 he became Professor of the English Language at Leeds. In the same year he published, with E.V. Gordon, his critical edition of *Sir Gawain and the Green Knight*, a poem which epitomizes medieval aristocratic life. On the strength of this as well as his previous work, he returned to Oxford in 1925, as Professor of Anglo-Saxon in Pembroke College. He retained this post until he retired in 1959. Most of his time was taken up with teaching and scholarship, the fruits of which included editions of *Beowulf*, the Anglo-Saxon heroic poem, and of the *Ancrene Wisse*, a medieval guide to meditation and spiritually, as well as two influential essays, "Chaucer as Philologist" (1934) and "Beowulf: the Monster and the Critics" (1936).

Finally in 1937 at age 45, Tolkien published his first work of fantasy. It was a children's story written originally for his own children, called *The Hobbit, or There and Back Again*. Although dependent on *The Silmarilion* for its background, its peoples, and its moral concerns, the story was much more unified and the style less solemn and more accessible.

As apologia for this effort and as a preview of things to come, Tolkien gave a lecture the next year at the Unviersity of St. Andrew's entitled "On Fairy-Stories." "Soon after *The Hobbit* was written and before its publication in 1937" (*FR,* viii) Tolkien began work on what was to develop in the *The Lord of the Rings* trilogy. In his letters during and after the Second World War, C.S. Lewis makes constant reference to the new work, chapters of which Tolkien read to the weekly meetings of the Inklings. The trilogy was not finally published, however, until 1954–55.

During that interval, he published only two short works of fantasy, the story "Leaf by Niggle" (1947), which dramatized his ideas on "subcreation," i.e., the creation of new, fantasy worlds, and "Farmer Giles of Ham," which combines elements of *The Hobbit,* e.g., the dragon and his hoard, with a sophisticated lightness of tone to achieve a truly charming success. A third work produced during this period, "The Homecoming of Beorhthnoth Beorhthelm's Son," is a dramatized commentary on the Anglo-Saxon poem *The Battle of Maldon* and is also very useful for understanding the system of social ethics embodied in the trilogy.

After the trilogy, Tolkien produced only two books. *The Adventures of Tom Bombadil* (1962) is a collection of poems most of which appeared in the trilogy and none of which can stand very well by itself. "Smith of Wooton Major" (1967), a saccharine children's story, forsakes Tolkien's characteristically direct action-adventure format for vague wanderings in Faerie and for a sugar-sweet sentimentality.

After retiring from teaching, Tolkien lived quietly with his wife in the suburbs of Oxford, pursuing his scholarly and creative interests. He died in 1973.

After his death his son, Christopher, edited and published two volumes of Tolkien's unfinished works, *The Silmarilion* in 1977 and *Unfinished Tales of Numenor and Middle-earth* in 1980.

6

J.R.R. Tolkien: The Early Stories

In his essay "On Fairy-Stories," Tolkien stated that his interest in fantasy dated from at least the First World War. Although his first work of fantasy, *The Silmarilion*, was near completion in the early 1920s, his first published work of fantasy, *The Hobbit*, was not written until many years later (it was not published until 1937). The germ of *The Hobbit* was a series of tales told to amuse his children. These stories concerned an imaginary world, Middle-earth, drawn largely from Tolkien's knowledge of Norse mythology and literature. Tolkien gave this world not just a history and heroic characters but imaginary languages and landscapes as well. Finally, with the urging of some of his colleagues at Oxford, he began preparing one of his tales for publication.[1] The product of that effort, *The Hobbit* bears the imprint of these multiple influences.

What emerged in *The Hobbit* is a marriage of Norse myth with the English children's story. The narrative concerns an extraordinary member of an extraordinarily ordinary race, Tolkien's little people, the hobbits. Hobbits are about half as tall as men (hence their other name, "haflings"), averaging two to three feet in height. Hobbits love to eat (six meals a day if they can get them) and to smoke (they invented it); they enjoy a good joke and a drink at the pub. They are also great enthusiasts for family history. Hobbits, however, are just a trifle too attached to their own comfortable, settled (Tolkien calls it "prosy") way of life, and they never give a thought to the wide world beyond their own small corner of it, the Shire. So far we are reminded of the idyllic life, unhampered by material care, of Kenneth Grahame's characters in *Wind in the Willows*.

But adventure suddenly bursts into the placid life of one particularly respectable hobbit, the wealthy Mr. Bilbo Baggins. He receives a visit from an old wizard named Gandalf who unexpectedly tells Bilbo that he wants him to go on an adventure, with a group of dwarves. Bilbo learns that many years before, a wealthy kingdom of dwarves located in a mountain far to the east had been attacked and destroyed by a terrible dragon named Smaug (a figure which Tolkien derives from the Norse dragon Fafnir, the guardian of the Nibelung hoard). Only a few of the dwarves, one of them Thorin, the grandson of the dead king and the leader of the dwarves assembled in Bilbo's kitchen, managed to escape the devastation. Now, however, he wants to return to the mountain and recover the treasure from the dragon. Gandalf proposes that he take Bilbo along to help him steal it. Bilbo is flabbergasted at first, but when the dwarves scoff at him, he plucks up his self-esteem, gathers up his courage, and sets off with them. On the way, they have many adventures. At first, Gandalf's magic is called upon to save the company several times, but eventually Bilbo takes over the leadership of the company and brings them safely to the mountain. During the journey, Bilbo finds a magic ring (derived from the Ring of the Nibelungs) which makes its wearer invisible. With its aid, he is able to steal a piece from the hoard. But the dragon soon discovers the theft. He seals their path of escape, trapping Bilbo and the dwarves in the mountain, and flies off to destroy the town where Bilbo and his friends had gotten help and supplies. The town is destroyed but the dragon is killed. The king of the wood elves, learning of the dragon's death and dreaming of the unguarded hoard, sets out with a large army for the mountain. Discovering the plight of the townsmen, however, he turns first to aid them. Meanwhile Thorin establishes himself as king under the mountain, but hearing of the approach of the elf-king's army, he sends for aid from Dain, his relative in the North. The spell of the hoard is upon him. He barricades himself in the mountain and refuses to give any gold to aid the townspeople in their time of need, even to return the wealth which belongs to the heir of Girion, king of Dale, a city of men which flourished at the foot of the mountain until the coming of the dragon. Fearing a battle, Bilbo tries to make peace between the various factions. But worse trouble is afoot. The lure of the treasure has drawn great armies of goblins and wolves from the mountains in the north and west. Just in time Gandalf is able to alert everyone to the real danger and to marshall the forces. After a fierce battle, in which Thorin proves his valor and dies, the wolves and goblins are all destroyed. Thorin is succeeded by his more open-handed relative Dain, and the dwarf kingdom is rebuilt. The threat from wolves and goblins is ended in that part of the world for many years. With Gandalf for a companion Bilbo returns home, but with his reputation for respectability irreparably damaged.

The story of Tolkien's *Hobbit* is organized around two basic motifs: the *bildungsroman* and the hoard. The first of these involves the development of the hero from one level of being, a shallow, domestic, hobbity sort of being, to another. Bilbo starts the journey as bewildered "confusticated" Mr. Baggins, the dwarves' employee, and winds up not only as leader of the dwarves but also as a shaper of human destiny.

The presence of the *bildungsroman* as one of the organizing themes of the novel is unmistakable. When we first meet him, Bilbo is a very unprepossessing character. As soon as he discovers that his visitor is Gandalf the wizard, he exclaims, "Dear me! Not the Gandalf who was responsible for so many quiet lads and lasses going off into the Blue for mad adventures. Anything from climbing trees to visiting Elves—or sailing in ships, sailing to other shores! Bless me, life used to be quite inter—I mean, you used to upset things badly in these parts once upon a time. I beg your pardon, but I had no idea you were still in business" (*H*, 19). Yet Gandalf still thinks him the right individual for a certain project he has in mind. As Gandalf tells the reluctant dwarves, "There is a lot more in him than you guess, and a deal more than he has any idea of himself" (*H*, 31). Of course, Bilbo is very uneasy, "flummoxed," and "bewuthered," notwithstanding Gandalf's apparent confidence in him, but we might well remember at this point the diffidence which characterized Ransom at the beginning of his adventures in C.S. Lewis's *Perelandra* or David Balfour at the beginning of *Kidnapped;* it is there to be overcome. Bilbo, after all, does have some pluck, and after hearing one of the dwarves remark that he looks more like a grocer than a burglar, determines to prove himself. And eventually he succeeds.

But first he must suffer danger and adversity. For instance, the dwarves begin to gain a new respect for him after he tells them of his audacity and daring in escaping from Gollum and the goblins in the mines of Moria. Part of this description is bluff, of course, for he doesn't tell them of his discovery and use of the magic ring, which confers invisibility on its wearer.

Soon, however, he is able to prove himself even to the reader. The decisive change comes when, lost in the Mirkwood and separated from his companions, Bilbo battles and kills one of the giant forest spiders. Afterwards, he feels himself to be a different person, "fiercer and bolder," despite his empty stomach.

As a result of this change, he becomes more active and authoritative. He decides to look for his companions, who had been captured by the giant spiders, and soon discovers them carefully guarded and trussed up in spider webbing. He slips on the ring, and singing a song of defiance, is able to lead all but one of the spiders away from the dwarves. He doubles back, kills the lone guard, and sets about freeing the dwarves. Before he can finish, however, the other spiders return. There is a desperate battle, in which Bilbo takes the leading part, before he and his comrades finally escape.

At this point in the adventure, Bilbo assumes command of the company. The dwarves now look to "little" Bilbo to determine their goals and their direction. Tolkien comments that the dwarves "had changed their opinion of Mr. Baggins very much, and had begun to have a great respect for him (as Gandalf had said they would)" (*H*, 163). Their faith in him is augmented when they are captured by the king of the wood-elves, and Bilbo conceives and effects still another rescue. Later it is he who remembers at exactly the right moment about the key which will unlock the side door to the mountain. It is he who steals a golden cup from the dragon's hoard, he who matches wits in a riddling contest with the wily (of course!) dragon, he who discovers the dragon's weak spot, an intelligence which comes eventually to Bard, the man who slays the dragon, and finally he who prevents war among men, elves, and dwarves. When Gandalf meets Bilbo again in the camp of Bard and the elf-king, he reiterates the statement, which at the beginning of the journey had been merely a statement of faith but by now has become a statement of fact, "There is always more about you than anyone expects" (*H*, 258).

What they expect of him is the Baggins side of Bilbo's personality—slow, conservative, eminently respectable. The Bagginses had lived in the neighborhood of the Hill for a very long time indeed and had become so predictable that their neighbors always knew what they would say before they even asked them. A Baggins never did anything adventurous or unexpected. What Bilbo's companions actually (and quite unexpectedly) get, however, is the Took part of Bilbo's character. His mother was a Took, and the Tooks were always great ones for adventures and consorting with elves. There was even a strong heroic strain on that side of Bilbo's ancestry. Bilbo's great-, great-, great-granduncle, one Bullroarer Took, had fought in a war against the goblins and had himself beheaded the goblin king.

Thus, Bilbo's personality is an unstable mix of respectability and adventurousness, domesticity and heroism, prosiness and poesy. The two sides are constantly warring with one another, and, even in the midst of his adventures, Bilbo has to restrain and beat down "his least Tookish part." For example, as he approaches his first encounter with the dragon, he says to himself, " 'Now you are in for it at last, Bilbo Baggins. . . . Dear me, what a fool I was and am!' said the least Tookish part of him" (*H*, 205). This interior dialectic might easily remind us of several of C.S. Lewis's characters. It is a sign of the propensity which both Lewis and Tolkien exhibit for conceiving of situations primarily in ethical terms. What Tolkien says of Bilbo as he prepares to meet the dragon, that "He fought the real battle in the tunnel alone" (*H*, 205), Lewis might have said of Ransom or of Digory Burke, the magician's nephew. Yet how Tolkien resolves this dialectic is very unusual in the literature of the *bildungsroman*.

Whereas Lewis crowns Ransom as Pendragon, king of Logres, whereas Stephen Dedalus becomes the godlike artist, Bilbo returns to his comfortable little home in the Shire. He has satisfied his thirst for adventure (not unlike the Pevensies at the end of *Prince Caspian*) and returns refreshed and complacent to his domestic routine. He has gotten the Took out of his system. Of course, he still visits elves, he even writes poetry, and he will never be "respectable" again. But as Gandalf tells him several years after the end of his adventure, he is again just a "little fellow." For, when Gandalf recounts to him the great changes for the good that have occurred in the land about the mountain, he exclaims,

"Then the prophecies of the old songs have turned out to be true, after a fashion!" "Of course," Gandalf replies and reminds him that other forces have had a hand in his destiny. His miraculous escapades and escapes were not simply the product of luck or chance. The fact that Bilbo has lost sight of these other forces indicates that he does not have the necessary breadth of understanding to comprehend the strange and portentous events to which he was party. "You are only quite a little fellow in a wide world after all!" says Gandalf, to which Bilbo can only reply with a laughing, "Thank goodness!" (*H,* 286–87).

He had once been an agent, a shaper of history, but in the end he is quite content to have the old prophecies fulfill themselves without his aid. Tolkien's choice of the word "little" at this point is crucial. It signifies a childlike passivity, which characterizes the Shire as a whole. The Shire is an extremely unheroic environment—Tolkien observes that axes are used for chopping wood and not goblins, and that shields are used as cradles and dishcovers and not in battle. Thus, when Tolkien uses "little" throughout the book to describe Bilbo, we sense that he is preparing us for this final withdrawal of Bilbo's self-determination, and conversely that he is afraid that once Bilbo is set on the path of self-determination, he will get out of hand.

This insecurity is revealed, in another way, by the presence of Gandalf. Most *bildungsromans,* whether *Wind in the Willows* or *Portrait of the Artist as a Young Man,* utilize the natural instincts of the hero to set the story in motion. Bilbo, however, sets out on his adventure only as a result of the insistence of Gandalf. It is not too much to say that the office of Gandalf is to offer Bilbo a vocation, a kind of religious call. Gandalf, after all, is a wizard, a figure traditionally invested with quasi-religious connotations. Moreover, he is benevolent, whimsical, and when occasion demands, incredibly powerful. He is Tolkien's all-purpose father-figure, patriarch, fond father, and Jupiter all in one, and it is on his authority that Bilbo may proceed on his adventure. Thus, if it is a novel of self-development, it is hedged at the beginning as well as at the end.

Just how much Bilbo develops in the direction of self-determination may be noted in his attitude toward that other primary motif of the novel, that emblem of pride and the temporal power which riches bring, the dragon's hoard. When Dain, Thorin's successor, offers Bilbo a portion of the hoard as reward for his efforts, Bilbo rejects the offer. He has seen the dangers which possession of the hoard entails, and he is quite willing to leave these dangers to a different breed of men, men fashioned for rule by their heredity and training. He is content merely to provide for his own comfort. Yet for Tolkien, this hobbit-sense represents a moral norm as well as the ultimate in political realism.

Only the Light-elves of the Last Homely House, where the company rests for a while during its journey, are similarly resistant to the spell of the hoard. Almost all the other characters in the story, however, come under its spell, and to the extent that they succumb, the more vicious and depraved they are, Smaug, of course, is the ultimate example of such depravity. He has absolutely no practical use for the gold and jewels which he guards so jealously; yet he steals and murders for their possession. Like other dragons, he is the quintessential parvenu—comments Tolkien, "[Dragons] hardly know a good bit of work from a bad, though they usually have a good notion of the current market value" (*H*, 35). In a similar vein, we notice that he neither sows nor reaps; he is the perfect parasite. He is content to fatten off the labor of others. We might suppose that he represents for Tolkien what Chesterton has called "the sins of capitalism."

Many other characters are similarly affected by the curse of the hoard. The goblins, for instance, ride to war in a bootless attempt to wrest the hoard from the dwarves. Gollum displays the same kind of disease. Once a hobbit like Bilbo, he is transformed into a murderous and dangerous creature of the dark by his lust for the ring. A valiant dwarf like Thorin can also come under the spell of the hoard. After the death of the dragon, Thorin spent a great deal of time in the treasure room, and, as a result, "the lust of [the hoard] was heavy on him" (*H*, 25). There is something in the gold that brings out the worst in even "the Good People," the wood-elves. "If the elf-king had a weakness, it was for treasure, especially for silver and white gems; and though his hoard was rich, he was ever eager for more" (*H*, 164). The Master of the Lake-town is also susceptible to the lure, especially since he had already given himself over to considerations of trade and wealth, a habit which was responsible for his eminent position. Eventually he runs away with the gold sent by Bard and Dain to rebuild the city of the Lakemen and dies in the swamps.

Contrasted with these characters on whom the treasure acts as curse, disease, and bewitchment, are the characters who either leave it, like Bilbo and the elves, and those—on them is dependent one of the important political wishes of the book—who are able to manage it for everyone's benefit, Dain and Bard. For as Bilbo tells Smaug, there is a curse on the treasure, and it must be handled very carefully lest it destroy its owner. "Surely, O Smaug the unassessably wealthy, you must realize that your success has made you some bitter enemies" (*H*, 215). The obvious solution to possession of the hoard, as practiced by Bard and Dain, is free-handedness and liberality to one's neighbors and friends. More than this, they embody a dynamic concept of leadership. While the master of the town runs for the safety of his boat, Bard organizes the battle against the dragon. He is a reincarnation of the heroic ideal figured in *Beowulf,* valour in battle and generosity to his thains, and a repudiation of the chamber-of-commerce types who figure so largely in contemporary politics.

Acting as reinforcement to this contrast of characters are contrasting image patterns of bounty and death. As lust for gold turns people into monsters, so it turns their world into a wasteland. The Desolation of Smaug is particularly well described:

> There was little grass, and before long there was neither bush nor tree, and only broken and blackened stumps to speak of ones long vanished. They were come to the Desolation of the Dragon, and they were come at the waning of the year.... Nothing moved in the waste, save the vapour and the water, and every now and again a black and ominous crow. The only sound was the sound of the stony water, and every now and again the harsh croak of a bird. (*H,* 196)

I think he would do well to hear echoes of T.S. Eliot, for as the landscapes in "The Wasteland" are *paysages moralises* so in *The Hobbit.* Tolkien's art may be best described as architectronic. As an artist he is interested not in fine writing or brilliant insights but in the arrangement of his materials into morally coherent patterns. As much as the *Hobbit* is about the growth of a character or the disposition of the hoard, it is the story of the conquest of light over dark, of order over chaos. There is almost none of Lewis's abundant delight in nature in Tolkien's fantasy. Tolkien holds his descriptions at two poles, the wild and the orderly, the desolate and the cultivated, the dark and the light. Thus we are prepared for the Desolation of Smaug by earlier ones. The waste associated with Smaug spins out and becomes associated with other landscapes, other peoples, and finally with a moral condition which underlies them all. The wild where they are nearly eaten by trolls, the mountains where they are captured by goblins, as well as the Mirkwood display this fundamental similarity to the dragon's waste. Here is the Mirkwood:

> It seemed to the hobbit that a silence began to draw in upon them. Birds began to sing less. There were no more deer; not even rabbits were to be seen. By the afternoon they had reached the eaves of Mirkwood, and were resting almost beneath the great overhanging boughs of its outer trees. Their trunks were huge and gnarled, their branches twisted, their leaves were dark and long. (*H,* 136)

In contrast to these chaotic districts are the orderly precincts of the Shire and the Last Homely House of the Light-elf Elrond: "His house was perfect, whether you liked food, or sleep, or work, or storytelling, or singing, or just sitting and thinking best, or a pleasant-mixture of them all. Evil things did not come into that valley" (*H,* 61). Besides these domestic precincts, there are also those aspects of nature which are benevolent and orderly, the eagles and Beorn, who hate goblins and wolves. It is no accident, then, given the deliberate patterning of the novel, that the climax of the novel is not the recovery of the hoard nor even the death of the dragon, but the Battle of Five Armies, in which these lights and darks arrange themselves on opposite sides and fight it out to a finish. In this repect, as in many others, *The Hobbit* is very similar to the *Lord of the Rings* trilogy. With the destruction of the forces of evil, darkness, and chaos, there is peace and order throughout the realm for a while.

In this conflict we can often sense the presence of a force which is important also in the trilogy, a force hinted at in Gandalf's final words to Bilbo. "You don't really suppose," he asks Bilbo, "that all your adventures and escapes were managed by mere luck, just for your sole benefit?" (*H*, 86). As Gandalf suggests, fate, good fortune, or in its Christian denomination, Providence, is a major actor in the story. The first of many happy chances occurs in the house of Elrond, as Gandalf, Thorin, Bilbo, and Elrond are gathered around the treasure map. Secret letters suddenly appear beside the more ordinary letters of the map. Elrond explains the letters and the company's great good fortune in being able to read them. They can only be seen in the light of a moon of the same shape and the same time of year as when they were written. They give the exact time of day and season and the exact phase of the moon, the conjunction being necessary to open the secret door in the mountain which leads to the treasure room. "[They say] stand by the grey stone when the thrush knocks and the setting sun with the last light of Durin's Day will shine upon the key-hole" (*H*, 62).

Much later, when Bilbo and his companions arrive at the mountain, they are stymied at first in their attempts to open the door. Only when Bilbo sees a thrush cracking open a snail on a grey stone does he remember Elrond's words. As the sun sets over the mountains, throwing a last ray on the door, suddenly a flake of stone falls from the door uncovering the keyhole. They are free to enter. But as they afterwards realize, it is only once in a very great while that such a conjunction occurs.

And these are not the only clues that the enterprise of Bilbo and the dwarves is being smiled upon. For what appear to the characters as inconveniences or disasters often reveal themselves as uncommon good fortune. After the near disaster with the trolls, they find in the trolls' cave elf-swords which stand them in good stead in their encounter with the goblins. Frodo is lost and terrified in the goblin caves and nearly meets death at the hand of Gollum, but fortunately he finds the ring, which besides rendering him invisible to Gollum and aiding his escape from the goblins is so useful on the later stages of the quest. But as Tolkien says when he first finds it, "It was a turning point in his career, but he did not know it" (*H*, 76). The same kind of fortunate chance—or in this case, mischance—occurs when the dwarves are captured by the wood-elves. Frodo conceives the desperate plan of bundling the dwarves in empty barrels and floating them out of the elf-king's palace on the river which rises in its lowest reaches. Bruised and frozen, the dwarves finally reach the city of the Lake where they receive aid. Certainly it is a desperate adventure from start to finish, but as Tolkien explicitly tells us, the river was actually the only safe way out of the forest.

The most striking instance of what we might call the irony of history, the way things develop contrary to human intention, is Thorin's summons to his relatives in the north. The raven comments cryptically but wisely on the action, "I will not say if this counsel be good or bad . . . but I will do what can be done" (*H,* 246). Thorin's intention is wholly selfish, to save the whole hoard for himself, but as it turns out, the dwarf army which arrives at his command is absolutely vital for the defeat of the goblins and wolves, and for the establishment of order and harmony afterward.

The structure of the novel is absolutely dependent on the presence of such good turns. Whether these are achieved by an invisible hand or by human daring or by a combination of both, they provide the relaxation of tension which is one of Tolkien's characteristic effects. The other quite naturally is the evocation of terror and the development of tension until it reaches a crescendo and one of the turning points. The book is an alternating series of contractions and relaxations, of ups and downs with relaxation, peace, and order predominant in the end. We remember his insistence on "Consolation" and on the presence of dyscatastrophe to balance and give salience to eucatastrophe.

These, then, are the major themes of Tolkien's first fantasy, a book which has never been out of print since it was first published and which, since the success of the trilogy, has become something of a children's classic in its own right. And one has to admit that it is a very attractive book. Tolkien's sense of a situation's potentiality for terror is particularly acute. The description of the dragon waste, which we have already examined, sets a tone of uneasiness and underlying terror with wonderful economy and force. Though they don't measure up to Lewis's witches, the goblins, wargs, and spiders are good fairy-tale villains. Much more sophisticated and effective is Tolkien's dramatization of the effect the hoard has on the dwarves. Finding the dragon away, they throw caution completely to the wind and wander in a daze all over the pile stuffing themselves with jewels and fitting themselves with costly armor. While they blithely ignore the danger, the reader experiences all the terror of the dragon's imminent return. It is obvious that this effect is consciously striven for, for Tolkien places the story of the dragon's death (an intelligence which would spoil the suspense) *after* this episode.

Another effect which Tolkien manages very well is humor. The opening scene, in which the flustered hobbit is eaten out of house and hole by the completely unconcerned dwarves, is especially fine. Moreover, the comedy turns on a particularly fine piece of observation. While Frodo expects to be treated as host and benefactor, the dwarves see him as a prospective employee who ought reasonably court their favor. Tolkien even engages on occasion in pure whimsy as with his description of Bullroarer Took's conquest of the goblin king. He "knocked their king Golfimbul's head clean off with a wooden club. It sailed a hundred yards through the air and went down a rabbit-hole, and in this way the battle was won and the game of Golf invented at the same moment" (*H*, 30). This juxtaposition of the horrific and the humorous, in fact, is one of Tolkien's most successful strategies. For instance, the riddling between Gollum and Bilbo is funny in a very serious and scary way. Gollum's last riddle is enough to raise the hair on anybody's head:

> This thing all things devours:
> birds, beasts, trees, flowers;
> gnaws iron, bites steel;
> grinds hard stones to meal;
> slays kings, ruins towns;
> and beats high mountains down. (*H*, 84)

And for his life, Bilbo cannot think of the answer. He worries and frets trying to remember all the monsters he had every heard about, but he realizes that none of them is right. Sitting in the dark, he can only see Gollum's eyes as he paddles through the water toward Bilbo. He is frightened to death, and "his tongue seem[s] to stick in his mouth; he want[s] to shout out: 'Give me more time! Give me time!' But all that [comes] out . . . [is]: 'Time! Time!' " (*H*, 84–85). And, of course, that is the right answer!

Bilbo's taunting of the dragon works in much the same way. After one successful foray, in which he brings away a gold cup, Bilbo ventures a second time down the corridor which leads to the dragon's lair. As he stops at the entrance, he sees that this time the dragon is waiting for him. "Well, thief! I smell you and I feel your air. I hear your breath. Come along! Help yourself again, there is plenty and to spare!" But Bilbo can spot a trap and counters with a particularly engaging lie. "No thank you, O Smaug the Tremendous! I did not come for presents. I only wished to have a look at you and see if you were truly as great as tales say. I did not believe them. . . . Truly songs and tales fall utterly short of the reality, O Smaug the Chiefest and Greatest of Calamities." To which the dragon responds in kind: "You have nice manners for a thief and a liar. You seem familiar with my name, but I don't seem to remember smelling you before. Who are you and where do you come from, may I ask?" "You may indeed!" answers Bilbo, warming to the game. "I come from under the hill, and under the hills and over the hills my paths led. And through the air, I am he that walks unseen. . . . I am the clue-finder, the web-cutter, the stinging fly. . . . I am he that buries his friends alive and drowns them and draws them alive again from the water" (*H*, 212–13). All these names refer, of course, to adventures he has encountered on his quest, but they are delightfully successful in disarming and distracting the ever-dangerous dragon. And even if Bilbo finally oversteps his luck, it is the kind of mistake which gives him character and endears him to us. Just as Bilbo is about to leave, he says "Well, I really must not detain Your Magnificence any longer, or keep you from much needed rest. Ponies take some catching, I believe, after a long start. And so do burglars" (*H*, 216). The dragon spouts a terrific flame at him for that last remark, singeing his hair badly, but the reader still feels it was worth it.

And since terror and humor are so much a part of his book, we feel that Tolkien's *Hobbit* is worth it. It is only when he is called upon to present the positive side of life that his vision wears thin. His description of hobbit life, of course, is good but his affection for it is mixed with a certain amount of irony. When Tolkien has to present a positive side of life, when he has to celebrate something, he is at a loss. Bilbo's two weeks in the house of the good elf Elrond are disposed of in a sentence. "Now it is a strange thing, but things that are good to have and days that are good to spend are soon told about, and not much to listen to; while things that are uncomfortable, palpitating, and even gruesome, may make a good tale, and take a deal of telling anyway. They stayed long in that good house, fourteen days at least, and they found it hard to leave" (*H*, 60). C.S. Lewis would have treated dinner at Beorn's house with a good deal more relish than Tolkien can muster, regaling us with names and descriptions of all kinds of savory food. Tolkien provides lean fare. "There they had a supper, or a dinner, such as they had not had since they left the Last Homely House in the West and said good-bye to Elrond." His attempts at charm and fun are similarly meager. "Indeed for a long time they could get nothing more out of Gandalf, he was so busy sending smokerings dodging round the pillars of the hall, changing them into all sorts of different shapes and colours, and setting them at last chasing one another out of the hole in the roof" (*H*, 130). "All sorts of different shapes and colours" is the shadow and not the substance of good writing.

There are other flaws to *The Hobbit*. A sense of the geographical surroundings, which is one of the strong points of his later work, the trilogy, is occasionally glossed over:

> At first they had passed through hobbit-lands, a wild respectable country inhabited by decent folk, with good roads, an inn or two, and now and then a dwarf or a farmer ambling by on business. Then they came to lands where people spoke strangely, and sang songs Bilbo had never heard before. Now they had gone on far into the Lone-lands, where there were no people left, no inns, and the roads grew steadily worse. Not far ahead were dreary hills, rising higher and higher, dark with trees. On some of them were old castles with an evil look, as if they had been built by wicked people, Everything seemed gloomy, for the weather that day had taken a nasty turn. (*H*, 43)

This is as abstract and unsubstantial as the fairy landscapes of George MacDonald or William Morris. In *The Lord of the Rings* and in *Wind in the Willows* our sense of the reality of this new world of possibility and fantasy is heightened by the author's efforts to make the new and the old worlds inhabit the same physical space. Here, however, we do not feel we are moving in a realm physically contiguous with the Shire. We pass from one to the other with too great a jolt.

What is more disappointing, however, is the way in which the *bildungsroman* is finally frustrated. It is simply not enough that Bilbo get the Took out of his system. We expect the hero of a *bildungsroman* to change and to retain the stature he has acquired during the course of the novel. *Wind in the Willows* is so much more charming simply because Mole is allowed to develop spontaneously. Mole displays an increasing knowledgeableness and sureness of character which mark him at the end of the story as a better individual than he was at the beginning. It is almost sad when Bilbo sinks back into his old, hobbity ways.

Although *The Hobbit* is in many ways a much happier and much lighter work than *The Lord of the Rings,* although it has a much happier ending, we can already sense Tolkien's dismay at political reality. It is an area of human activity dominated by lust for the hoard and its consequent conflicts. Tolkien's hero is content to take only what he needs, though he might have very much more. Political power is left to the heroes who are great enough and good enough to wield it.

Yet Tolkien's descriptions of these very heroes betray his fundamental political pessimism. They are, quite simply, too good to be true. This is connected with Tolkien's inability to effectively create a positive side of life; his pessimism is so deep. His real interest is in characters like Bilbo, who are unable to cope with political society. His heroic characters are shadowy and unconvincing. If, as Gunnar Urang maintains, Tolkien's hope for the modern world resides in "the power and authority" revealed in a character like Bard, then Tolkien has very little hope indeed.

In his 1938 essay "On Fairy-Stories," delivered the year after the publication of *The Hobbit* as an Andrew Lang lecture at the University of St. Andrews, Tolkien attempts to legitimate his use of the fairy story to convey his particular vision. This involves basically the legitimation of wish-fulfillment as the highest pleasure of literature. The fairy story becomes the refuge for those motifs and functions of heroic and mythic literature which have been discarded at the advent of realism. If well written, its primary value, of course, will be as literature, but the fairy story also offers, "in a peculiar degree or mode, these things: Fantasy, Recovery, Escape, Consolation." In this analysis we note that Tolkien is already moving away from literature conceived strictly for children, for these are "all things of which children have, as a rule, less need than older people" (*TR,* 46).

Fantasy, says Tolkien, is an act of the imagination much higher than the realistic, which merely replicates the world it has before its eyes. Fantasy enables the writer to engage in what Tolkien calls "sub-creation." Fantasy discovers new worlds, worlds of "arresting strangeness" which it develops with "the inner consistency of [seen] reality." (We should note that Tolkien is one of the most important sources for C.S. Lewis's theorizing about fantasy.) Tolkien says that fantasy is the power of invention at the heart of all mythology; "in such 'fantasy,' as it is called new form is made: Faerie begins; Man becomes a sub-creator" (*TR,* 22). Tolkien warns us that, of course, one must not mistake one's own creation ("secondary reality," he calls it) for the Primary Reality of the Creator, but he tells us also that such is this great privilege of human nature, that even in its abuse man reveals the divine origin of his nature.

The second thing fairy stories do better than realistic kinds of fiction is to recover a relationship with nature which has been lost not only because of man's sinful state but also because of the development of vast scientific technologies. Fairy stories insist on the need for humility in the face of nature. We cannot really hold or own anything, for it is not really ours. We are reminded of the biblical concept of stewardship. It is one of the informing concepts of Tolkien's morality. The following quotation ought to remind us as well of Bilbo's warning to the dragon. "Creative fantasy... may open your hoard and let all the locked things fly away like cage-birds. The gems all turn into flowers of flames, and you will be warned that all you had (or knew) was dangerous and potent, not really effectively chained, free and wild; no more yours than they were you" (*TR,* 59). "Recovery" ought to leave one "poor in spirit" even if it doesn't make him poor in body as well.

Thirdly, Tolkien claims that fairy stories allow one an Escape from "our present time and self-made misery" (*TR,* 69). Unlike the realist, the escapist is not concerned with "the whims of evanescent fashion." He has "more permanent and fundamental things" to talk about, like "lightning, for example" (*TR,* 61).

Finally, the fantasist offer us consolation for "other things more grim and terrible to fly from than the noise, stench, ruthlessness, and extravagance of the internal-combustion engine. There are hunger, thirst, poverty, pain, sorrow, injustice, death. And even when men are not facing hard things such as these, there are ancient limitations from which fairy-stories offer a sort of escape, and old ambitions and desires... to which they offer a kind of satisfaction and consolation" (*TR,* 65–66). For these reasons men in fairy stories visit the deepest seas or fly like a bird or hear the speech of animals. But most important of all is the consolation of a "Happy Ending." It is that *eucatastrophe,* that joyous turn which denies universal final defeat and gives us a fleeting glimpse of joy, "Joy beyond the walls of the world, poignant as grief."

But more than evoking an emotional reaction in the reader, "the peculiar quality of the 'joy' in successful fantasy can thus be explained as a sudden glimpse of underlying reality or truth" (*TR,* 70–71). In fact, Tolkien here used the term joy much as Lewis uses it in his autobiography, not just as an emotion but as evidence for a theory of history, a morality, a theology, an eschatology, and a metaphysics. "In the 'eucatastrophe' we see in a brief vision that the answer may be greater—it may be a faroff gleam or echo of *evangelium* in the real world" (*TR,* 71). And to confirm the fact that this is the essence of the Christian story, he says, "The Gospels contain a fairy-story, or a story of a larger kind which embraces all the essence of fairy-stories. . . . But this story has entered History and the primary world; the desire and aspiration of sub-creation has been raised to the fulfillment of Creation. The birth of Christ is the eucatastrophe of the story of the Incarnation. This story begins and ends in joy" (*TR,* 71–77). This is finally why the joy of fairy stories is superior to the somberness of realism. Realism is not really real. But in the fairy story, "Art has been verified. God is the Lord, of angels, and of men—and of elves. Legend and history have met and fused" (*TR,* 72).

This essay is obviously very important for understanding Tolkien's religious commitment and his political concerns. The interesting thing, though, is to notice how far his own artistic practice, especially in *The Lord of the Rings,* diverges from the formulas he states in this essay. If the reader escapes the pressures of everyday life, it is only by immersing himself in a work which is particularly evocative of the same kind of pressures and dangers. There is nothing of Never-never Land in Tolkien's trilogy. Moreover, the consolation he offers us is of the most tentative sort. The victory over evil is not permanent and the losses involved in that victory are very great. Even *The Hobbit* has elements of sadness which mar the "happy ending." Perhaps only his short story "Farmer Giles of Ham" comes close to filling the demands of the formula, but even there, there is little hint of the "Joy beyond the wall of the world," which is the burden of true consolation.

Although not published until nine years later, the story "Leaf by Niggle" is actually a companion piece to the essay "On Fairy-Stories," written at almost exactly the same time (1938–39). Tolkien points up this relationship in the introduction to his book *Tree and Leaf,* published in 1965, which combined the two works in one place for the first time. "Though one is an 'essay' and the other a 'story,' they are related: by the symbols of Tree and Leaf, and by both touching in different ways on what is called in the essay 'sub-creation'" (*TR,* 2). In the essay he writes of the "Tree of Tales" whose seed may be planted in almost any soil. It is this "Tree" which ultimately determines the pattern of each of the leaves, i.e. stories, but each story is to be read and enjoyed not only for its reflection of the basic pattern but also for its own ineradicable uniqueness. "Each leaf, of oak and ash and thorn, is a unique embodiment of the pattern, and for some this very year may be *the* embodiment, the first ever seen and recognized, though oaks have put forth leaves for countless generations of men" (*TR,* 56). In other words, contemporary writers can make new and significant contributions to a tradition which reaches back to the roots of human experience.

The nature and extent of that contribution are the subjects for "Leaf by Niggle." The story concerns an obscure "little man," a modern Everyman, named Niggle. The first thing we learn about him is that he has a long journey to take for which he is making at best desultory preparations. The second is that he is an aspiring but not successful painter. He is kept busy with other things, especially with his neighbor, Parish. Now Niggle is not a man to shirk his duty or even to complain unduly, but he cannot help but feel that his painting is somehow more important than his social responsibilities. Before he can make much progress on his projected masterpiece, however, "the Inspector" arrives to start him on his journey and to upbraid him for his laxness in carrying out his duty. Niggle is taken away to the Workhouse, where he is worked so hard he forgets his physical misery and his confinement and achieves inner peace. One night while lying in his cell, he overhears two voices—one severe, the other gentle—debating his fate. Finally on the recommendation of the second voice, he is released from the Workhouse and taken to a peaceful countryside very like the one pictured in his last painting—only this is for real. "Nothing needed altering any longer, nothing was wrong, as far as it had gone, but it needed continuing up to a definite point" (*TR*, 105). He realizes that to continue to work he is going to need Parish's help, and sure enough Parish, released from the Workhouse as a result of Niggle's kind words on his behalf, arrives to help him. Together they finish the work, which they call Niggle's Parish, and while Parish waits for his wife, Niggle walks into the mountains beyond his country, "always uphill." In an epilogue we return to Niggle's old community where the Councillor and the Schoolmaster debate Niggle's worth to society. The Councillor maintains that it is only "old-fashioned stuff. Private day-dreaming." But the Schoolmaster remarks that "I can't get it out of my mind." "Out of your what?" asks the Councillor. But the Second Voice, whom Niggle had heard in the Workhouse, interrupts this scene to confirm the Schoolmaster's opinion. "It is proving very useful indeed, as a holiday, and a refreshment. It is splendid for convalescence; and not only for that, for many it is the best introduction to the Mountains. It works wonders in some cases. I am sending more and more there. They seldom have to come back [to the Workhouse]" (*TR*, 112).

One of the most interesting things about this story is its affinity with medieval Christian artistic forms. Tolkien's most important works, *The Hobbit* and *The Ring,* involve a deliberate suppression of Christian allusions. In "Leaf by Niggle" his content and forms as well as the deep structure of the story is specifically Christian. It is a story of spiritual progress framed in a barely disguised allegory—not unlike some in Lewis. It also contains the time-tested medieval form of debate and its main character and initial action, i.e., the impending journey, consistently evoke the important medieval morality play, *Everyman.*

Nevertheless, its discontinuities with medieval forms are as important to the structure and meaning of the story as its continuities. These discontinuities indicate the area in which Tolkien inserts his notions on subcreation, that god-like spark in man, into the domain of ascetic Christianity. The story thus attempts to find a place for the artist in the Christian community. The story is organized around the tension between the dreamy, mystical, and artistic Niggle and the various embodiments of practicality he encounters, from Parish, to the Inspector, to the harsh voice in the Workhouse, to finally the Councillor. Ultimately this is a tension between justice and mercy, the Father and the Son. In keeping with the new dispensation of mercy inaugurated by the Incarnation, the second, gentler voice is able to appreciate and understand Niggle's artistic passion, Niggle's great urge to create a wholly adumbrated artistic world. Niggle is a subcreator and his creativity itself points to the existence of spirit and a spiritual reality which transcends the narrow positivism of the Councillor. It is an example and instruction for others. As the Schoolteacher says, "I can't get it out of my mind." Of course, Niggle's artistic bent is too one-sided. He has to learn to seriously attend to his own garden (his personal, spiritual plot) and to his Parish (his involvement with the community of Christians). Hence the two stages of his purgatory: Workhouse and Parish. But because it mirrors divine creativity and because it is didactically useful ("it is the best introduction to the Mountains"), Tolkien is able to find an honored place for artistic creation in the Christian scheme of things. At the end of the story, the two aspects of the psychic territory are joined; art is revealed as useful while the humdrum reveals its hunger for the visionary. Those who would separate them and denigrate the one or the other are repudiated. Tolkien repudiates the philistine as well as the aesthete.

Yet Tolkien has conquered new ground for a Christian aesthetic, and it is precisely in the realm of the aesthete. For Niggle is anything but a Christian artist, at least in the received sense. His is not a religious topic. He is not elucidating man's progress toward God or reconciling God's way to man. His subject, like that of the Romantics, is "Nature"—which may or may not be the visible manifestation of God. Moreover, the art—unlike his life—has no extraneous object; it seeks only its own perfection. In fact, the only aspect which his work shares with Christian theology is its idealism—its flight from modern "reality" as envisioned by the Councillor. Yet it is precisely this visionary quality, which is the soul and substance of Niggle's artistic activity, which redeems it from a Christian point of view. For Tolkien, it betrays the presence of a spiritual principle in man which transcends his earthly condition; it positively refutes modern scientism and positivism. Hence Tolkien's conviction that fantasy "is, I think not a lower but a higher form of Art, indeed the most nearly pure form, and so (when achieved) the most potent" (*TR,* 47).

If Tolkien's story does succeed in embodying the polemical content of his essay, nevertheless it doesn't make a very good story. Tolkien is too committed to the authority of the Catholic Church to realize how authoritarian and stultifying are the relations he pictures between Niggle and the Inspector or between Niggle and the authorities in the Workhouse. Tolkien insists that "the laws in his country were rather strict," but he wants us to realize that these laws are good because they keep Niggle from becoming too abstracted from reality, e.g., Parish. (In this story Tolkien does not make a distinction between God's law and the state's; there seems at times to exist in his mind a simple correlation between divine order and state bureaucracy, hence the choice of the title "Inspector" for his Death.) Yet after Niggle's experience in the workhouse, an extension and rationalization of those "interfering" laws, he realizes their beneficence. He develops a sense of self-discipline and a certain satisfaction in doing socially useful work. Yet what freedom is gained is purchased at the price of complete renunciation of will and of self. Moreover, this is an ideology whose political face is complete aquiescence in the status quo. The Workhouse is described more as a prison than a hospital, its attendants unfriendly, its appearance austere, its rules capricious. It suggests a kind of living death, and yet Niggle's total submission to legitimate authority is the ultimate lesson of Tolkien's fable.

If this seems to be merely a theoretical objection, it also has artistic implications. Niggle is a mere cardboard figure, a puppet manipulated by forces outside of himself. There is nothing he can do or choose but take his medicine. This lack of concreteness is also reflected in the very schematized character of the action—from fallible existence to Workhouse to Parish to mountains. They are simply four different places connected only by the railroad and by Tolkien's insistence that they represent a spiritual progression. That is to say, their relation is only theoretical and not actualized. They indicate a progression only by virtue of the Christian practice implied everywhere in their author's writing. The Inspector, for example, represents the intrusion of a "higher" spiritual reality into Niggle's everyday life. But this fact is supplied only by the author's intention, by his forcing of the materials into a historic frame.

For example, the Councillor, the one villain in the piece, and the Inspector, the representative of a divine order, evince very similar attitudes toward creative work. Just as the Inspector upbraids Niggle for neglecting the repair of his crippled neighbor's house and suggests that he should dismantle his masterwork and use the materials for the repair, the Councillor complains that Niggle is a "silly little man" with no practical or economic use. And when the Councillor suggests that people like Niggle need to be forced into some useful job, like washing dishes in a communal kitchen, we might justifiably feel that we are not very far at all from the Workhouse. In other words, we are totally unconvinced by Tolkien's presentation that the Inspector/Workhouse represents a higher authority than the Councillor. Tolkien's conception of authority founders in its own contradictions: temporal authority reflects divine spiritual authority, hence laws are useful and necessary; but the temporal lawgiver is narrow-minded and philistine, hence the introduction of a higher lawgiver; but he is the mirror-image of the temporal authority; hence the invocation of a spiritual discipline whose activity and wisdom is beyond the ken of fallible humanity, of a providence after the fact; but this discipline is as cruel and repulsive as anything invented by the most monstrous temporal authority (it reminds one of nothing so much as brainwashing); the only thing that can be said for it is that Niggle comes to accept it; but by then he is a lobotomized cipher, his freedom and creativity so hemmed and hampered that it is finally merely abstract.

Tolkien's next story, "Farmer Giles of Ham," published some eleven years after the writing of "Leaf by Niggle," is cast in a completely comic mode. Unlike *The Hobbit* or *the Lord of the Rings* it is a true fairy tale, for it displays a happy ending much less qualified than those of either of the other stories.

The plot itself has many similarities to that of *The Hobbit*. The story concerns a prosperous farmer named Giles, who did his business well, enjoyed good company and good talk, but had little taste for what his author calls "memorable events" (what Tolkien calls "adventure" in *The Hobbit*). Like Bilbo in particular and hobbits in general, he gave very little thought "to the Wide World outside [his] fields, the village and the nearest market." For all his skill at "keeping the wolf from the door: that is, keeping himself as fat and comfortable as his father before him," however, he keeps stumbling into adventure's path.

Like Bilbo, Giles is a very low hero. He bears none of the intense ethical concerns that burden Frodo. Like Bilbo, he is capable of rendering important services to the community, but he accomplishes these more by accident than by intention. Thus, he acquires his reputation in the community, and his consequent responsibility to deal with the dragon, by a stroke of dumb luck.

One night a giant wanders into his farm. Giles, hearing the ruckus, terrifiedly sets on the giant with his blunderbuss. Thinking it the sting of a large unfriendly insect, the giant returns to his mountain haunts.

By sheer dumb luck, Giles wins a great reputation in the community for this feat of daring and receives from the king a magical sword from his valor. But the trouble with a reputation is that it brings responsibilities, and when the next danger to the community appears, it is Giles who must deal with it. It is interesting to note that neither Bilbo nor Giles (nor even Frodo) is what one expects as material for a hero. In either case, the force of someone else's expectations is what sets them on the path to real heroism. It is almost as if these expectations themselves were capable of effecting a change of character.

Thus after his encounter with the giant, people began to think of him less as a prosperous and unassuming farmer and more as a heroic giant-killer. And Giles begins to think in those terms as well.

Thus when new trouble, the "cunning, inquisitive, greedy, well-armoured, but not over bold" dragon, Chrysophylax Dives, arrives, Giles is much more ready to deal with it. But like Bilbo he is more gifted with shrewdness than with strength. Covering his armor and sword with a large cloak, he sets off in humble guise in search of the dragon. He surprises the dragon with his magic sword and it does the rest, completely daunting the worm. Giles chases the distracted villain until, exhausted, it collapses in the village square. It promises to pay for its rampages and to give rich presents to every inhabitant of the village. It sets out for its mountain lair, however, with not a thought of returning.

The king, hearing of the dragon's promise, rushes to Ham thinking to claim the hoard for his empty coffers. When the dragon fails to return, the king is more furious than all the rest. He orders Giles to join an expedition to punish the dragon and gather his hoard. The haughty knights who comprise the main force of the expedition disdain the help of this lowborn farmer. But the courtiers, whose thoughts are only of etiquette, honor, and precedence, turn out to be not much good in a fight. For when the dragon attacks them, some are killed immediately, "before they could even issue their formal challenge to battle," and the rest turn in terror and flee. Giles, however, whose horse has gone lame, must face the dragon. Furtunately the dragon remembers the terrible sword and is terrified enough to part with a good deal of his hoard. Giles sets out, with the dragon carrying the loot on his back. On the way Giles hires a small army of trustworthy young lads at "good wages," not unlike the Connecticut Yankee. Finally he returns to a rejoicing Ham and retires quietly with the treasure to his farm. When the king hears of his return, he sends for Giles and the treasure. But Giles refuses, and the king sets out with a picked company to punish the rebel. Giles, however, is completely sure of himself by this time, and when the king demands the sword as well as the treasure, Giles retorts with taunting solemnity, "Give *us* your crown." The dragon aids him in vanquishing the king's knights, and Giles establishes himself as ruler of the Little Kingdom, formed by Ham and its environs. He rules wisely and justly.

The first thing we notice about the story is that like *The Hobbit* it concerns the development of the main character. But unlike *The Hobbit* this development is placed in an ironical context. Giles never approaches the stature of his idol, the great dragon slayer Bellomarius, whose magical sword he wields. The sword itself does most of the fighting. Giles's accomplishments always have an element of luck in them. Nevertheless Giles takes control of his social destiny in a way that is impossible for Bilbo and later for Frodo. In fact, one may see the story as a very gentle parable of the transition from feudal to bourgeois society. The kingdom is falling into ruin and decay. The bravery and exploits which in olden days lifted the name of Bellomarius to every lip have decayed. Only arrogance and parody are spawned in the present generation of courtiers.

It takes a *nouveau* like Giles, who embodies virtues of shrewdness and practicality but also some courage, to meet the danger. In fact, for all his lowborn interest in material comfort, Giles is truly superior to the products of the court. He is shrewd and adaptable. They are only interested in honor and formality. For example, after the dragon has brought out a huge pile of treasure, he tells Giles that he has barely enough to keep himself respectable. Giles allows him to keep the rest in return for the dragon's help in carting Giles's part of the treasure back to Ham. Giles has struck the best possible bargain, and showed what Tolkien calls "laudable discretion." "A knight would have stood out for the whole hoard and got a curse laid upon it. And as likely as not, if Giles had driven the worm to despair, he would have turned and fought in the end, Tailbiter or no Tailbiter" (*R,* 64).

We should remember that "Farmer Giles" was composed in the midst of Tolkien's work on the trilogy. Yet it comes the closest of anything that Tolkien has written to presenting a view of political society essentially different from the pessimistic one hinted at in *The Hobbit* and openly described in *The Lord of the Rings.* For the only time in his career as a writer, does Tolkien completely abandon the myth, embodied in Bard and Aragorn, of the born leader, noble and heroic, and suggest that the practicality and resourcefulness of a lowly bourgeois might become the basis of a social order.

Perhaps he wanted to take a rest from the high seriousness and rigorous artistry of *The Ring.* This is not to say that *The Ring* doesn't have its light moments; but these only counterpoint the generally serious and somber tone. As a whole, "Farmer Giles" represents the farthest Tolkien ever went in the direction of pure whimsy. What he gives us is a delight to read, with a completely refreshing lightness of tone. This tone is set at the very beginning, in a foreword in which Tolkien, almost reminding us of a Nabokov or Borges, assumes the mask of a sententious and antique scholar and mocks the pedantry to which Tolkien's own profession is all too susceptible.

> An excuse for presenting a translation of this curious tale, out of its very insular Latin into the modern tongue of the United Kingdom, may be found in the glimpse that it affords of life in a dark period of the history of Britain, not to mention the light that it throws on the origin of some difficult place-names. Some may find the character and adventure of its hero attractive in themselves. (*TR,* 7)

The condescending smile in that last sentence is worth the price of admission. This lightness of tone is maintained and expanded in his description of the giant. Reversing the fairy tale stereotype of malevolent and destructive giants, his giant is a blundering innocent, more clumsy than malevolent. He is a cousin to the well-meaning but incompetent giants of Narnia. The choice of epithets to describe him is particularly amusing. No "sacker of cities" but "the ruin of roads" and "the desolation of Gardens," he is more a natural principle of entropy than a spirit of cosmic malevolence.

The description of the dragon is managed along much the same lines. He is "not over bold." While Giles is holding Tailbiter, he is as manageable as a kitten. If he is as cunning, he is far less dreadful a threat than Smaug, the dragon in *The Hobbit*. His rampage does not lead to a fearful desolation. Instead it becomes the pretext for an unwonted whimsy as Tolkien seeks to avoid the potential horror of the situation. One particularly felicitious moment:

> The next day the dragon moved to the neighboring village of Quercetum (Oakley in the vulgar tongue). He ate not only sheep and cows and one or two persons of tender age, but he ate the parson too. Rather rashly the parson had sought to dissuade him from his evil ways. (*TR*, 30)

Not only are we presented with the amusing spectacle of the simple but pious pastor becoming a just dessert, but we are also given a truly delicious pun—we suspect that these aforesaid young persons are tender as veal.

A further example of this droll but highly amusing wit is revealed in Tolkien's metaphorical transformation of the king into a dragon. We have been suspicious all along that the king is a little too concerned with his exchequer, but when Tolkien tells us that the king, angered at Giles's refusal to deposit the hoard in the royal treasury, "rode off in a fiery anger," and that on viewing the farmer's house, "he had a mind to burn the place down," we realize that like Eustace in Lewis's story *The Voyage of the Dawn Treader*, he has lived too long with his dragonish thoughts.

One final instance of this tone: the old king is vanquished and Giles rules supreme over the Little Kingdom. It is a happy and prosperous place and Tolkien bids farewell to it with jollity and jest. "His wife made a queen of great size and majesty, and she kept a tight hand on the household accounts. There was no getting round Queen Agatha—at least it was a long walk" (*TR*, 75). It is an old joke, but a happy one.

In conclusion, "Farmer Giles of Ham" is the lightest but in no way the least important of Tolkien's stories. It attests to his versatility as a writer and suggests that those critics who, like William Ready, see only somber morality and heroic pessimism in his work haven't read his work closely enough. Even in *The Lord of the Rings*, which most closely approximates Tolkien's sense of the pessimism and heroism of Norse mythology, there are many such moments.

Published in 1953, "The Homecoming of Beorhtnoth Beorhthelm's Son" is a remarkably straightforward exposition of those principles of social organization and social ethics which pervade not only Tolkien's view of English chivalry but also the world he creates in the *Ring*. It is divided into three parts: first, an introductory note describing the historical background and content of the famous Anglo-Saxon poem "The Battle of Maldon"; second, a short verse drama, composed in imitation of Anglo-Saxon alliterative verse, in which an old man, Tidwald, and a lad named Torhthelm meet on the battlefield after dark to recover the body of their earl; and third, an essay which explicates the Maldon poet's attribution of the word "ofermod"—"overmastering pride"—to the earl and situates the poem in the literature of medieval chivalry.

"The Battle of Maldon" tells the story of the earl Beorhtnoth, who, while leading a small defense force against a Viking raiding party in 991, made a deplorable error of judgment and allowed the invaders to cross a narrow causeway from the island they occupied to the mainland and there engage Beorhtnoth's English force in open combat. "This act of pride and misplaced chivalry proved fatal. Beorhtnoth was slain and the English routed; but the duke's 'household,' containing the picked knights and officers of his body-guard, some of them members of his own family, fought on, until they all fell dead beside their lord" (*TR,* 4).

The verse drama which follows this introduction acts as a dramatic comment on the action just described. Both Tidwald and Torhthelm agree that it bodes ill for the future. "The roads are rough and rest is short/ for English men in Aethelred's day" (*TR,* 17), says Tidwald, the older man. "It's dark! It's dark! and doom coming!" says Torhthelm, the younger and more poetic of the two. But Torhthelm is too much the dreamer and too apt to console himself with the cliches of chivalry. As in "Leaf by Niggle," we have a contrast between the practical and the poetic, only this time weighted on the side of the practical. In Torhthelm's imaginings Beorhtnoth becomes another Beowulf.

> Now mourn for ever
> Saxon and English, from the sea's margin
> to the western forest! The wall is fallen,
> women are weeping; the wood is blazing
> and the fire flaming as a far beacon.
> Build high the barrow his bones to keep!...
> Glory loved he; now glory earning
> his grave shall be green, while ground or sea,
> while word or woe in the world lasteth. (*TR,* 6–7)

"Good words enough, gleeman Totta!" Tidwald warns him. Present realities force us to dismiss the sleights of poetry. Tidwald also reminds us that Beorhtnoth's glory, if he should win it, is little good to the poor and lowly who will suffer at the hands of the invaders for his rashness.

It is Tidwald who speaks most sense, and who most fully recognizes the impact of the evil times. Yet Tidwald is not the normative consciousness of the piece. The answer to the troublous times is contained in the final bit of dramatic action; the appearance of a chorus of monks chanting over the bier of the slain earl, "Dirige, Domine, in conspectu tuo viam mean," "Direct my path in your sight, O Lord." The heroic code is not simply criticized on a natural level but transcended. It is not humans who are the final judge of man's glory but God. And He is not primarily concerned with great actions in battle but with keeping to the duties of one's station in life.

This becomes clearer in the section entitled "Ofermod." In it Tolkien develops a hierarchical theory of social relations. The rights and duties of the ruler are completely different from the rights and duties of the ruled. Beorhtnoth failed to treat his duty seriously enough. He was responsible for the safety of the realm and the lives of his retainers, but he lost sight of these great aims and instead threw away his life and the lives of his men on what amounted to a sporting match. Yet Tolkien's criticism extends to more than this one act and implies a criticism of one very important aspect of the heroic tradition. Tolkien distinguishes the "strictly heroic" from its excess, the chivalrous, i.e., in which temporal honor or fame is itself a motive. Beorhtnoth had been misled by the "aristocratic tradition" of the poets into performing acts which were motivated by the desire for temporal honor and fame but which violated his real obligations and duties. Thus, when Tidwald dismisses the poet's babblings, he is criticizing the cultural tradition which had formed, and deformed, Beorhtnoth.

Yet if Beorhtnoth was guilty of a grave misjudgment, his retainers were in no way released from their obligation of love and loyalty. On the level of the subordinate, the rules of conduct are completely different. They are duty-bound to obey their lord, regardless of his rashness. In fact, Tolkien feels that the Maldon poet's criticism of Beorhtnoth only adds to the stature of the retainers. It is only in the subordinates of medieval literature, the young Beowulf, the retainers of Beorhtnoth, and Gawain, that we find the licit development of the chivalric spirit. Only they can say: "Will shall be sterner, heart the bolder, spirit the greater as our strength lessens." For the rulers, for Beowulf the king, Beorhtnoth, Arthur (and in Tolkien's own fiction, Aragorn), is the task of keeping matters from reaching such a pass. Ultimately Tolkien sees the heroic code as an attempt to balance two contradictory needs—the desire for personal glory and the demand for social stability.

In these statements we recognize a temperament fully as responsive to the appeal of social hierarchy as Lewis's. In fact, this has important consequences for the constitution of the action and society of the Ring. First of all, the two basic plot elements, the epic and the quest, mirror the fundamental dichotomy between ruler and ruled. The task of the epic hero, Aragorn, is to destroy the threat to peace and order and to restore the kingdom. This he does with all due perspicacity and care, with a regard not only for his subjects but also for himself as the locus of kingship. The task of the quest-hero, Frodo, involves no such scruples. He is entirely reckless of self. Second, this schematization becomes the basis of the entire world of social relations in the *Ring*. The relations of Frodo and Sam, master and servant, are enough to convince us of this. Frodo tries to keep Sam from too great a danger in much the same way that Aragorn tries to protect his kingdom; and Sam risks himself at every turn for his master in the same way that Frodo risks everything for his duty.

J.R.R. Tolkien: *The Lord of the Rings*

That most of the attention focused on Tolkien should be concentrated on the trilogy, *The Lord of the Rings,* seems only natural, not only because of its scope, its monumental size, and ambition, but also because of the actual achievement of the work. Yet we should not lose sight of the fact that the basis for many of the achievements of the trilogy is laid solidly in his earlier fantasy, especially in *The Hobbit. The Lord of the Rings* returns to the invented world first presented in *The Hobbit,* but this time presents it in much greater range and detail.

The story of *The Lord of the Rings* has two important threads. The main plot relates the quest of Bilbo's heir, Frodo Baggins, to destroy the Ring of Power, which Bilbo had found during his journey in *The Hobbit* but which was originally fashioned by "the Dark Lord," Sauron, for his own evil purposes. The subordinate plot concerns the quest of Aragorn, heir to the throne of a southern kingdom named Gondor, to defeat the legions of the Dark Lord and to establish himself as king.

In our analysis of *The Hobbit,* we noticed a structure composed of moments of tension followed by moments of release and relaxation. This organizing principle is continued in the trilogy but with a difference which makes it a much more compelling experience. For every time tension begins to build, it starts on a higher level. As the book develops, the dangers are greater, the odds riskier, the desired good more urgent. This crescendo is enhanced by the fact that the book has a much greater sense of finality than *The Hobbit.* All the action builds to the climax when Gollum and the ring fall into Mount Doom, thereby eliminating the threat of Sauron forever from Middle-earth. A climax is not so clearly emphasized in *The Hobbit.* Neither Bilbo nor the dwarves have any idea at the beginning that their search for the gold might lead to the Battle of Five Armies. But from the second chapter of the Ring, we know what Frodo must do, and the suspense involved in waiting 1,300 pages for him to accomplish it is a very important factor in our response to the book.

What Lewis essays only sketchily—in *That Hideous Strength* and in *The Last Battle*—and then retreats from rapidly becomes the essential moment of

Tolkien's vision, the apocalyptic tension between good and evil. This feeling for cataclysm, for the threat of violent change, is what marks Tolkien's fantasy as specifically modern and gives it that contemporary relevance which Gunnar Urang presses so hard to establish.[1] Yet his trilogy is not a "sign of hope," as Urang claims, that the present situation of gross misuse of political power, and of rapid development in destructive technologies will get better, but rather a sign that the situation is so bad. Tolkien is not concerned with discovering a Christian alternative (as, for instance, a writer like Lewis is) to the lived situation, but in elucidating its evils and the heroism which, knowing its doom, attempts to overcome those evils. Here, as nowhere else in his writing, is the Norse influence so strong. What Tolkien says of the author of *Beowulf* might also be said of himself: Despite the fact that he is a Christian, "Its author is still concerned primarily with *man on earth*. . . . Yet this theme would not be so treated, but for the nearness of a pagan time. . . . He could view from without, but still feel immediately and from within, the old dogma: despair of the event, combined with faith in the value of doomed resistance" (*BMC,* 73). Surely if Tolkien himself had not lived in a "pagan time"—a time torn by wars, in which he himself participated and which threatened the destruction of all "culture" and "civilization"—he would not find *Beowulf* so attractive as a scholar and so significant as an artist.

In fact, for all the similarities between *The Lord of the Rings* and *The Hobbit*—and they include elements of structure, tone, plot, and character—the two books are very different in overall effect. *The Lord of the Rings* is much closer to *Beowulf* than to *The Hobbit.* Thus, while *The Hobbit* is a balance of humour and terror, *The Lord of the Rings* is generally a much more somber work. The birthday party which Bilbo gives himself at the beginning of the trilogy is obviously a parallel to the party for the dwarves at the beginning of *The Hobbit.* Like the earlier party it displays a similar lightness of tone. Hobbits, on their birthday give presents to their guests, and Bilbo "gave away presents to all and sundry—the latter were those who went out again by the back way and came in again by the gate" (*FR,* 60). In a similar vein is Tolkien's observation that "The invitations were limited to twelve dozen (a number also called by the hobbits one Gross, though the word was not considered proper to use of people)" (*FR,* 52). But as soon as Bilbo slips on his magic ring, to the utter dismay of his dinner guests, the tone changes. Frodo, Bilbo's heir, who knows of his plans to leave the Shire, can't help but feel sad. "He felt deeply troubled; he realized he loved the old hobbit dearly" (*FR,* 56). This shift in tone is enhanced by the change we see in Bilbo. In *The Hobbit* he had been a quick-witted, happy-go-lucky fellow for whom the ring was a toy to be played with. But long years of possessing the ring has taken its toll; the sinister effect of the ring (a point not explicitly made in *The Hobbit*) is very apparent by now. "I am old, Gandalf. I don't look it, but I am beginning to feel it in my heart of hearts. . . . Why I feel all thin, sort of *stretched,* if you know what I mean: like butter that has been scraped over too much bread. That can't be right. I need a change or something" (*FR* 58). But when Gandalf asks him to leave the ring behind for Frodo as he had promised, he gets angry, and tells Gandalf, in what is a direct echo of the evil Gollum, "It is mine, I tell you. My own. My precious. Yes, my precious." Thus, by virtue of these new developments, the ring acquires the same sinister connotations as the dragon hoard in *The Hobbit.* Moreover, the evil of Gollum is seen as merely the result of the much more sinister influence of the ring. Finally, it is this shift in tone in the very first chapter of the trilogy which sets the mood for the rest of the work.

For Tolkien's concerns have shifted a great deal from those of *The Hobbit.* In our analysis of *The Hobbit* we noticed the controlling motifs of that work to be the *bildungsroman* and the hoard. In the trilogy the career of Frodo as Ringbearer and main protagonist of the novel represents a genuine departure from the role played by Bilbo in *The Hobbit.* Moreover, we notice in the ring itself an extension of the same moral evil implied by the hoard, only this time on a scale involving the whole political and social fabric of Middle-earth. Unlike the hoard, the ring cannot be managed for good ends. It must be destroyed.

In *The Hobbit* we notice that the quest-hero and the great political event at the end of the book are not directly related. From the viewpoint of the *bildungsroman* Bilbo is the book's most important character. In this light, the dangers implied by "the wild" (goblins, wolves, dragons, et al.) are of secondary importance. They are the foil against which he displays his wit, cunning, and courage, the backcloth from which he emerges to dominate the first sections of the book. But these forces of darkness are not met and destroyed by Bilbo; in this sense he is only a minor hero. Bard, the dragon slayer, and Dain, the dwarf general, stand as the book's real epic heroes and their exploits, or rather the battle itself, completely dominates the last section of the book. As a matter of fact, Bilbo completely disappears; he is knocked on the head in the midst of the battle and it is only some time afterward tht he learns of the battle's outcome. If there is a serious structural flaw in *The Hobbit,* it is that the two motifs somehow don't quite seem to meet. Bilbo reaches a certain point in the action, but somehow the action gets completely out of his hands and has to be taken over by others. It is this tension that is figured in the discrepancy between Bilbo and Bard. Perhaps this is the same problem that Lewis encounters in *That Hideous Strength* where his heroes, the ones on whom he has focused all his moral and imaginative interest, do nothing to eliminate the evil but just sit back at the climax and let the angels do their work.

The Lord of the Rings, on the other hand, does not have this kind of problem. We know exactly how the various forces relate and which event is most important. By making the ring the chief danger to the stability and peace of Middle-earth and by making its destruction the primary responsibility of the hero, the book avoids the split between public and private which damages *The Hobbit.* The trilogy portrays a completely politicized world; there are no sanctuaries, as in *The Hobbit,* from the contest for power. The Shire itself is invaded and its tranquility destroyed when Saruman, the renegade wizard, establishes an industrialized police state. Thus the attention which Tolkien gives to the great public events, the councils of war, the preparations and battles themselves, or to the development of the book's most important public figure, the king of Gondor, Aragorn, is not unconnected with the career of the Ringbearer. For ultimately the fate of the wars as well as Aragorn's kingship and the future political destiny of Middle-earth hinge on the success or failure of Frodo's quest into Mordor. After the victory before the gates of Minas Tirith, the various leaders of the forces arranged against Mordor assemble to determine their next move. Gandalf tells them that their only chance is to distract Sauron from Frodo, his true danger. It is their duty to sacrifice themselves and draw Sauron's forces out of Mordor and his attention away from Frodo. Only in this way can Frodo make his way through Mordor to Mt. Doom and destroy the ring.

For within the ring itself are all the dangers and ambiguities which Tolkien sees in the wielding of temporal power. The ring is the ultimate extension of the human will. It can make its wearer invisible, with all the advantages that accrue from seeing without being seen. It grants a kind of immortality (not unlike that given by the cosmic fire to She in H. Rider Haggard's novel; in fact, *She* is the only recent work which Tolkien will admit as having influenced him). Moreover, the wearer of the ring can force other people to submit to his will. Yet these are all advantages with a dubious side. Isolation, the strain which we observe in Bilbo, and a tendency to see a threat wherever there is a free will, all work to create a monster where there had been a person. Gandalf says of Sauron that "the only measure that he knows is desire, desire for power; and so he judges all hearts" (*FR,* 353). In fact, nobody can wear the ring for long without becoming in turn a tyrant very much like Sauron. Thus, as Elrond, a leader of the good elves, tells Frodo, they cannot use the ring itself against Sauron.

Saruman, for instance, who had once been chief of the Council of Good Wizards, had succumbed to the temptation of power, and had betrayed the Wise and thrown in his lot with Sauron. The only hope for Middle-earth is to destroy the ring, thereby preventing anyone from ever gaining control of its power again. Thus, a crucial difference between this story and *The Hobbit* is its complete pessimism as to the ability of men to wield power. In *The Hobbit,* Bard and Dain had available measures which could neutralize the curse of the hoard. In the trilogy, it is as if the hero had to destroy the hoard in order to kill the dragon and end the curse.

This pessimism has profound implications for the rest of the work. Its impact on Frodo's career as quest-hero is especially noticeable. There are, of course, large similarities between the careers of Bilbo and Frodo. Like Bilbo, Frodo is chosen for his task by Gandalf. Like Bilbo, Frodo displays an initial reluctance in pursuing it. In the course of their novels, both become more imposing persons. At the end, both withdraw from the political and social concerns of Middle-earth.

Yet even at the beginning this similarity only emphasizes a fundamental difference. The benign atmosphere of *The Hobbit,* an atmosphere guaranteed not only by the avuncular narrator but also by the sweetness of the ending, is renounced for a tougher view of the hero's quest. It is no longer simply a matter of sending a timid little hobbit out into the wide world in order to prove himself as a political and social agent. The crucial difference between the quest of Frodo and that of Bilbo is that Bilbo's occurs in a public setting while Frodo's has a much more private setting. This is a matter of emphasis of course. Bilbo does engage in moral combat and struggles with himself on occasion. But he does other things as well. Frodo is almost exclusively involved with an interior struggle to determine whether he or the ring will rule. Bilbo's quest is that of the knight; Frodo's that of the saint. This accounts for the tremendous difference in tone between the two books. There is something happy-go-lucky in Bilbo which we do not find in Frodo. Frodo is much more like the Beowulf described in Tolkien's essay, "*Beowulf:* the Monster and the Critics." He says of Beowulf that "Something more significant than a standard hero, a man faced with a foe more evil than any human enemy of house or realm, is before us, and yet incarnate in time, walking in heroic history, and treading the named lands of the North" (*BMC,* 66). We see in Frodo an increasing gravity and solemnity of character. The physical pain and mental anguish, which constitute the tissue, bone, and marrow of Frodo's experience, is much greater than any faced by Bilbo. Of course there are times early on when, like Bilbo, he wishes himself completely out of the situation, but finally the danger and struggle make of him a new person. "For a moment it appeared to Sam that his master had grown and Gollum had shrunk: a tall stern shadow, a mightly lord who hid his brightness in grey cloud, and at his feet a little whining dog" (*TT,* 285).

We should, of course, realize that Frodo's development is much more complicated than Bilbo's. Bilbo's laments for the security of the Shire are merely Tolkien's way of preparing us for his relapse into hobbitry (a curious word, which reminds us of the resemblance between the words "hobbit and "Babbit"). Even though he develops into a more impressive person, Frodo is also capable of what, save for the pressure of the ring, could only be viewed as rashness and stupidity.

In particular, his relations with Gollum signal a new maturity. Sam, Frodo's faithful but impetuous servant, would have Gollum killed, but Frodo remembers a conversation he had had with Gandalf:

> What a pity Bilbo did not stab the vile creature, when he had a chance! [said Frodo]
> Pity? It was Pity that stayed his hand. Pity, and Mercy: not to strike without need. [said Gandalf]
> I do not feel any pity for Gollum. He deserves death.
> Deserves death! I daresay he does. Many that live deserve death. And some die that deserve life. Can you give that to them? Then be not too eager to deal death out in the name of justice, fearing for your own safety. Even the wise cannot see all ends. (*TT,* 281)

Although Gandalf is inventing a Bilbo different from the one we see in *The Hobbit,* the lesson he draws is clear enough. Frodo refuses to kill Gollum, thereby displaying a much greater moral stature than he had earlier. Moreover, as the quest goes on, Frodo displays unquestionably greater spunk and determination. After he has seen the effect his presence has on Boromir, who wants to take the ring to Gondor and use it against Sauron, he decides to leave his companions. This is the kind of self-reliance of which he was simply incapable at the beginning of the story. His reluctance at the beginning to set out from the Shire, his home, and his friends delayed him until he was almost captured by the servants of Sauron. As the quest progresses, he becomes less and less concerned for his own welfare and more committed to his duty. Finding the gates of Mordor heavily guarded, he purposes to walk in come what may. "His face was grim and set, but resolute. He was filthy, haggard and pinched with weariness, but he cowered no longer and his eyes were clear. 'I purpose to enter Mordor, and I know no other way. Therefore I shall go this way. I do not ask anyone to go with me'" (*TT,* 310). Moreover, we see that as Frodo nears Mordor, he is better able to resist the power of Sauron and his servants. Early in the journey, during a fight with Sauron's chief servants, the Black Riders, he had obeyed the command of the Morgul king, their leader, and placed the ring on his finger, thereby revealing himself to his enemies. Later, at the gates of the king's own city, Minas Morgul, he is able to resist that call.

This growth, however, is no guarantee that Frodo is completely capable of managing on his own. When Gandalf explains to Frodo why he had been chosen, he indicated that it was not a matter of Frodo's possessing any superior power or wisdom. We might say that it is a matter of his innocence; the powerful and the wise are even more susceptible to the influence of the ring, with its promise of complete power and mastery over others. But under the constant tension, Frodo's self-control sometimes slips. The chief example is when he rushes madly over the pass which leads to Mordor and is captured by Shelob. He and Sam had just escaped Shelob's first trap:

Wild joy at their escape from the very mouth of despair suddenly filled all his mind. His head whirled as with a draught of potent wine. He sprang out of the tunnel, shouting as he came. It seemed light in that dark land to his eyes that had passed through the den of night. The great smokes had risen and grown thinner, and the last hours of a somber day were passing; the red glare of Mordor had died away in sullen gloom. Yet it seemed to Frodo that he looked upon a morning of sudden hope. Almost he had reached the summit of the wall. Only a little higher now.... A short race, a sprinter's course, and he would be through.

"The pass, Sam!" he cried, not heeding the shrillness of his voice, that released from the choking airs of the tunnel rang out now high and wild. (*TT,* 422)

Almost immediately the unwary Frodo is seized by the crafty Shelob. This is an unusual moment. The language is extremely charged. After all this time we do not expect this sudden hysteria of Frodo, but it is Tolkien's way of reminding us of the power of the ring. Until the ring is destroyed, there is always the possibility that Frodo will betray himself.

But it is not simply a matter of betraying himself to an overwhelming yet exterior evil. Early on, during the fight at Weathertop with the Black Riders, Frodo succumbs to the bidding of the Black Riders and puts on the ring. Certainly he is responding to the pressure of the Black Riders. Yet we notice that this struggle is also with himself, with his own hobbity tendency to take the easy way out. It makes sense in terms of the geography of the book that the action here takes place while they are still very close to the Shire. Later on, he does not so easily succumb to this temptation. In Book 4 as they are about to cross the mountains which separate Gondor from Mordor, Frodo is again confronted by the call of the chief of the Ringwraiths. But this time he is able to sustain the attack. Moreover, as the journey becomes tougher, the hobbit's determination to carry out his task becomes firmer. In fact, as Frodo nears Mount Doom he becomes less and less like a hobbit and more and more like the evil he is trying to destroy. That is, as he approaches the dominion of terror and domination, the more his temptations become those of power and domination and less those of passivity and weakness. For example, in the last Book, Sam fears the effects of the strain on his master and offers to shoulder some of the responsibility, to carry the ring for awhile.

"No, no!" cried Frodo, snatching the Ring and chain from Sam's hands. "No you won't, you thief!" He panted, staring at Sam with eyes wide with fear and enmity. Then suddenly, clasping the Ring on one clenched fist, he stood aghast. Sam had changed before his very eyes into an orc, leering and pawing at his treasure, a foul little creature with greedy eyes and slobbering mouth. (*RR,* 230)

We remember the importance of distortions of sight in Lewis's books as signs of moral derangement. The very thing that happened to Bilbo after carrying the ring for many years, happens to Frodo as well.

Of course this is just preparatory to the moment when Frodo, in the very heart of the volcano, at the very instant when the quest could be successfully completed, chooses instead to assume the power of the ring for himself:

> "I have come." he said, "But I do not choose to do what I came to do. I will not do this deed. The Ring is mine!" And far away, as Frodo put on the Ring and claimed it for his own, even in Sammath Naur the very heart of his realm, the Power in Barad-dur was shaken, and the Tower trembled from its foundations to its proud and bitter crown. (*Rk,* 274–75)

At this moment, the crucial moment of the entire trilogy, Tolkien's profound pessimism about human nature and about political activity is revealed in all its depth. He has no faith at all in the efficacy of human activity to solve the fundamental problems of mankind. Like those medieval works he most admires, *Beowulf, Maldon,* and *Sir Gawain and the Green Knight,* his own work is a criticism of the concept of the hero. Compare Frodo with a character like David Balfour in *Kidnapped,* who like Frodo has little confidence in his ability to perform the task set before him but is nevertheless able to do it, and with a character like Beowulf whose vaunt is merely the prelude to his fall, and we see that in the crucial matter of performance Frodo is as inadequate as Beowulf. Yet unlike Beowulf or Beorhtnoth he does not succumb to a dragon or a band of Danes; instead he is more like Gawain, whose failure is a moral failure, a failure to honor his promise to his host. Frodo's failure is more serious, involving as it does the fate of Middle-earth, but it too is a moral failure. In Frodo's betrayal of his duty, Tolkien seems to suggest a very Christian observation, that human nature cannot solve its fundamental problems. This pessimism, of course, has tremendous political implications. Tolkien is saying that no one, not even the most innocent, is immune to the corruption of power. The realm of politics will always be one in which the lust for power is predominant. No considerations of duty or humanity will ultimately restrain the powerful from seeking even more power. Thus political life will always be marked by warfare. As C.S. Lewis says, "The text itself teaches us that Sauron is eternal; the war of the Ring is only one of a thousand wars against him" (*DP,* 15).

After the climactic events at Mount Doom, Frodo is a much changed person. He is no longer fit to live the life of an ordinary hobbit. He tells Sam, "There is no real going back. Though I may come to the Shire, it will not seem the same; for I shall not be the same. I am wounded with knife, sting, and tooth, and a long burden. Where shall I find rest" (*RK,* 331). He is much humbled. He no longer has any pretensions to power or greatness. Yet in his own way, Frodo has become a greater person than he had been before he left the Shire. Gandalf tells him and his companions on the quest, "You are grown up now. Grown indeed very high; among the great you are, and I have no longer any fear at all for any of you" (*RK,* 340). This work is much more clearly intended to be a *bildungsroman.* Frodo has left the Shire a hobbit and returned a saint. His suffering and his experience of the war of the ring has given him a profound horror of violence. In the battle to rid the Shire of Saruman and his followers, Frodo is a peacemaker. "Frodo had been in the battle, but he had not drawn sword, and his chief part had been to prevent the hobbits, in their wrath at their losses, from slaying those of their enemies who threw down their weapons" (*RK,* 365). But he is anxious to depart Middle-earth with its strife and suffering and scars. Finally he leaves with the elves for the Blessed Realm, where he can at last find respite from his wounds.

If Tolkien's pessimism begins with the concept of the hero, it extends even to the concept of Providence, the belief in the divine guidance of history. The accomplishment of Frodo's quest is left to no human agent but to fate, to the product of conflicting human intentions which transcends any one intention. (We remember the manifold ironies of *The Hobbit.*) For at the moment of dramatic reversal, when Frodo abandons the quest, another equally swift reversal—one of those eucatastrophes Tolkien talks so much about—takes place. Gollum, who has followed Frodo into the cave, attacks the hobbit, grabs his hand, and is able to bite the ring finger off. As he dances about waving his bloody token, he falls into the fiery chasm. The ring is destroyed along with the power of Sauron. The proud tower collapses. The quest is accomplished.

We remember Gandalf's words to Frodo, "Gollum may play a part that neither he nor Sauron has foreseen" (*FR,* 336) But compare them to Elrond's counsel to the assembled Fellowship of the Ring: "You have come and are here met, in this very nick of time, by chance as it may seem. Yet it is not so. Believe rather that it is so ordered that we, who sit here, and none others, must now find counsel for the peril of the world." Both speakers invoke a plan beyond the ken of mortals. Yet neither of these speeches involve a conclusive affirmation of Providence. The language is too circumspect. "Gollum *may* play a part." The sense that the fellowship is guided by a wiser hand than they know is a matter of *belief,* a working hypothesis whose primary function is to strengthen their resolve to perform their dangerous task. The tragedy of Sauron's victory is averted either by pure chance or by Providence, but neither we nor the characters in Tolkien's story can tell which.

The somberness of Tolkien's work is further intensified by the poignance and nostalgia of the ending. The Third Age of Middle-earth has come to an end, and Tolkien exploits fully the sense of loss evoked by an ending. For one thing, Gandalf and his kindred, the elves, must leave Middle-earth. With the destruction of the Ruling Ring, the power of the lesser elf-rings is diminished. Gandalf tells Aragorn, "Though much has been saved, much must now pass away; and the power of the Three Rings also is ended. And all the lands that you see, and those that lie round about them, shall be dwellings of Men. For the time comes of the Dominion of Men, and the Elder Kindred shall fade or depart" (*RK,* 208). This sense of loss is intensified by Frodo's departure. For all of Tolkien's insistence on the importance of eucatastrophe and consolation in defining the fairy story, his best fairy story is remarkable primarily for its pessimism and the sadness of its ending. We don't remember Sam's return home to his wife and child—as banal an existence as that with which Bilbo is left in *The Hobbit*—but the parting between Sam and the only real passion of his life, his master.

> To Sam the evening deepened to darkness as he stood at the Haven; and as he looked at the grey sea he saw only a shadow on the waters that was soon lost in the West. There still he stood far into the night, hearing only the sigh and murmur of the waves on the shores of Middle-earth, and the sound of them sank deep into his heart. (*RK,* 384)

It is a startling moment, one to which every reader can fully respond. The world at this moment is almost as dark as if Sauron had won—a curious reversal. By comparison, his assurance that Frodo will find peace in the Blessed Realm is not very convincing at all. We are reminded once again that like the *Beowulf* author, Tolkien is "still dealing with the great temporal tragedy" (*BMC,* 73).

Finally, we notice that, although the danger is overcome for the time being, it is sure to arise again in the future. This is the main message of the Appendices, which relate how over and over again in the history of Middle-earth the danger has been only barely overcome and at very grave cost. But even in the story itself, there is a very strong sense that all good things are passing and that all a good man can do is try to preserve them. As Gandalf tells Aragorn, "The Third Age of the world is ended, and the new age is begun; and it is your task to order its beginning to preserve what may be preserved" (*RK,* 307–8).

These, then, are the basic thematic concerns of the trilogy—the desparate conflict in which good is pitted against evil, the dangers of power, the inadequacy of the hero, the mystery of Providence, and the loss attendant upon the conflict. By themselves, they are the stuff of much literature, but they are handled with an authority and a sureness which makes Tolkien's work likely to last.

What is most striking on first reading *The Lord of the Rings* is our sense that somewhere Middle-earth must really exist. To some extent this is a result of the sheer size of the story. It seems the result of a plenitude of information that only reality could provide. First of all is Tolkien's firm grasp of the imaginary geography of his world. The maps, to which the reader must constantly refer, are just one outcome of his almost gritty sense of the reality of Middle-earth. The abundance of strange place names further adds to this opaqueness. But as the place names also indicate, we are moving not just in a geographically strange world but in a strange linguistic world as well. One of the obvious pleasures of the book is rolling the strange words around in your mouth: Gondor, perhaps suggests a condor, a picture of a large soaring bird among lofty mountains; and Mordor (from OE *mortor*, "murder") redolent of morbidity, rigor mortis, and morticians. If one were to sit down with an Old English or a Norse dictionary, one could discover exactly what many of the strange words mean. But even if one doesn't know exactly what they mean, they are still suggestive of a certain emotional tone. This is even more the case with Tolkien's invented languages which he sprinkles throughout the *Ring.* They are not so much imitations of real languages, as explorations of certain possibilities of sounds. This bit of Mordorian with its concatenation of low and back vowels (a, u) and plosive and sibilant consonants (s, z, g, k, p, b) seems to the very language of hell:

> Ash nazg durbatuluk, ash nazg gimbatul, ash nazg thrakatuluk agh burzum-ishi krimpatul.
> (*FR,* 27)

There is not an agreeable sound in the entire sentence. By speaking Tolkien's invented languages out loud, then, we might get a sense of the elfen or the dwarvish or the mordorian, but, more than this, we sense a world which resists our knowledge and desire.

This illusion of reality is also heightened by certain narrative techniques. Whereas in *The Hobbit* the structure of tension and consolation is basically straightforward, in the trilogy the structure is somewhat more complicated. For example, at a critical moment in the battle before Minas Tirith, the trumpet of Rohan is heard in the distance. But instead of immediately pursuing the rescue, Tolkien ends the chapter and shifts the scene to the Riders of Rohan, describing in a chapter with its own suspense how they were able to arrive at Minas Tirith in time. Now this is not incompatible with the consolation which Tolkien seeks to provide; quite the contrary. The delay heightens the illusion of reality, convinces us of the existence of an opacity which simple wish cannot overcome. It takes hard riding and skilled diplomacy to arrive at Gondor in time. In fact, the delay makes our sense of the eucatastrophe more real.

In his essay on *Beowulf,* Tolkien suggests that the use of historical allusions in *Beowulf* is to give "an impression of reality and weight; the story is not in the air.... it is part of the solid world" (*BAC,* 58). Tolkien's invention includes not just a geography but also a history to which he constantly alludes in the story, much of which is contained in the Appendices to the trilogy. Although entirely imaginary, this "history" performs much the same function as the historical allusions in *Beowulf.* It gives the illusion that "the story is not in the air." In fact, for the reader without specialized knowledge about Old English history and language, reading *The Lord of the Rings* is very much like reading *Beowulf.* In both, the "historical" allusions act as a fictional coefficient of reality.

Tolkien's world, however, is also the source of a completely different kind of pleasure. Besides being a "sub-created" world, it is a work which in many instances alludes to earlier literary texts. We experience a pleasure of recognition in his imitations and borrowing. The ring itself is pregnant with many literary associations, the chief of which are Wagner's *Ring* and the Norse Ring of the Nibelungs. Even such a minor detail as the fact that hobbits give presents on their birthday seems to be an allusion to the "heroic" custom of gift-giving. The possibilities for source-hunting seem almost unlimited with Tolkien—almost as good as those for Joyce. He was an immensely well-read man, and he seems to have brought all his experience as a reader to his task as writer. John Tinkler's article "Old English in Rohan" locates just one of the major areas of Tolkien's borrowings.

But for the ordinary reader, the main interest of Tolkien's trilogy lies in the figures and incidents which are most fully realized in their own terms, in those points at which the subcreated world is most dense. We have already noted that the chief of Tolkien's thematic concerns is the threatening presence of evil. It is no surprise, then, that his villains should be such good creations in their own right and capable of giving us the appropriate chills.

As early as Book 1, we get a striking picture of this kind of character. Frodo, pursued by a Black Rider, is hiding in some trees.

> The sound of hoofs stopped. As Frodo watched he saw something dark pass across the lighter space between two trees, and then halt. It looked like the black shade of a horse led by a smaller black shadow. The black shadow stood close to the point where they had left the path, and it swayed from side to side. Frodo thought he heard the sound of snuffling. The shadow bent to the ground, and then began to crawl towards him. (*FR,* 116)

The color imagery, the repeated "black," is too obvious to linger over. What is more interesting is the curious transformation of the standing creature, into a crawling, half-canine, half-reptilian creature. The phrase "it swayed from side to side" is particularly effective in not only suggesting in a very concrete way the onset of the transformation but also in suggesting the quasi-serpentine nature it assumes. Even more interesting is the fact that Frodo can't quite see this evil agency; all he can really perceive is a dark shadow. This sense of a threat, which we can't see but which can see us, is picked up again and again in the book.

This is especially true of Tolkien's ultimate villain, Sauron. During the course of thirteen hundred pages we never once see him. Yet his presence is felt throughout the journey. There is something very canny in Tolkien's refusal to disclose his villain. Many critics have noticed that he is so "terrifying" precisely because we never see him. Just as he eludes the other characters, he eludes the reader. We can not get a sense of him as a literary "character." He is not an object of literary perception in the same way that the other characters are. He is the fictional equivalent of subjectivity, embodying all the potential threat that such freedom involves. Moreover, he is completely "mysterious," and the unknown is always more frightening than the known.

Almost all we know about him—his power, his thirst for domination, his complete disregard for other beings—we know by inference, by the character of his domain, for instance:

> Here nothing lived, not even the leprous growths that feed on rottenness. The gasping pools were choked with ash and crawling muds, sickly white and grey, as if the mountains had vomited the filth of their entrails upon the lands about. High mounds of crushed and powdered rock, great cones of earth fire-blasted and poison-stained, stood like an obscene graveyard in endless rows, slowly revealed in the reluctant light. They had come to the desolation that lay before Mordor: the lasting monument to the dark labour of its slaves that should endure when all their purposes were made void; a land defiled, diseased beyond healing. (*TT,* 302)

This landscape portrays extremely well the material destruction and moral horror which accompany the lust for power. In particular it evokes Tolkien's experience of the Western Front in World War I. In fact, it has a concreteness and a "reality" which convince us of the authenticity—and to some extent, of the justice—of Tolkien's pessimism.

The same kind of revulsion is strongly present in Tolkien's description of Saruman's stronghold, Isengard:

> Once it had been green and filled with avenues and groves of fruitful trees, watered by streams that flowed from the mountains to a lake. But no green thing grew there in the latter days of Saruman. The plain was bored and delved. Shafts were driven deep into the ground; their upper ends were covered by low mounds and domes of stone, so that in the moonlight the Ring of Isengard looked like a graveyard of unquiet dead. For the ground trembled. The shafts ran down by many slopes and spiral stairs to caverns far under; there Saruman had treasuries, storehouses, armouries, smithies, and great furnaces. Iron wheels revolved there endlessly, and hammers thudded. At night plumes of vapour steamed from the vents, lit from beneath with red light, or blue, or venomous green. (*TT,* 203–4)

Tolkien's industrial landscape is just as harrowing as his landscape of war. As we notice in his affection for the green countryside of the Shire, Tolkien's instincts are pastoral, antiurban, and antiindustrial. Isengard, however is a kind of nightmare, but when the same thing happens in the Shire, the result is an unusual and striking poignance (not unlike the poignance which attends the end of the Third Age and the departure of Frodo and the Elves):

> It was one of the saddest hours in their lives. The great chimney rose up before them; and as they drew near the old village across the Water, through rows of new mean houses along each side of the road, they saw the new mill in all its frowning and dirty ugliness: a great brick building straddling the stream, which it fouled with a steaming and stinking outflow. All along the Bywater Road every tree had been felled. (*RK,* 366)

Here, as nowhere else, is Tolkien's nostalgia for an older England and his alienation from modern industrial England so strongly felt.

Besides creating convincing villains and wastelands, Tolkien is also a very good storyteller. We have already noticed how Tolkien's storytelling adds to the "reality" of his work. But it has another very important effect; Tolkien is a master of suspense. The suspense which Tolkien generates in his story is a prime ingredient of the generally somber world-view which emerges from his work.

We have noted earlier that the structure of *The Lord of the Rings* is composed of moments of building tension followed by moments of release. We have already noted one such instance. Frodo is hiding from a Black Rider, but the Rider is down on the ground sniffing him out. The tension builds, as the Rider gets closer. But suddenly the sound of Elvish voices reaches them, and the Rider quickly retreats. Like Frodo, the reader takes a deep sigh of relief.

This is what we might call "narrative suspense." Tolkien uses another device which we might call "structural suspense." It consists simply of stopping or suspending the action at a crucial moment. In fact, *The Lord of the Rings* may be compared to one of the old movie serials. It has six episodes and the first five end in a cliff-hanger. One of the most effective is at the end of Book 4. Frodo has been overcome by Shelob, but Sam is able to beat her off. To his horror he can see no sign of life in his master. Finally, he decides to take on his master's quest. He takes the ring from Frodo and starts over the pass. But when orcs gather around Frodo and start to carry him away, Sam changes his mind and decides his place is with his master no matter what. He follows the orcs up a dark tunnel, and overhears that Frodo is actually alive, only full of poison. Sam is overwhelmed at his folly in leaving Frodo. Maddened with the desire to free his master, he charges after the orcs. But too late; the door to their tower swings shut just as Sam rushes up. The Book ends thus: "The gate was shut. Sam hurled himself against the bolted brazen plates and fell senseless to the ground. He was out in the darkness. Frodo was alive but taken by the Enemy" (*TT,* 447). All throughout the following book, in which the first attack on Minas Tirith is repulsed (some two hundred pages), we are asking what is happening to Sam and Frodo.

As can be seen from this example, Tolkien intensifies the effect of this "structural suspense" by the use of another technique which reminds us of the movie art. At this crucial moment when Frodo is unconscious and in the hands of the enemy, Tolkien "cuts" to a completely different field of action. In fact, in Book 5 Tolkien has three and four different narrative strands going, and he keeps "cross-cutting" from one to another (after the manner of, say, D.W. Griffith in *Birth of a Nation*) to increase the suspense. Book 5 opens with Gandalf and Pippin riding to Minas Tirith. When they arrive, they join its forces in preparing for the siege. The scene then switches to Aragorn's ride through the Haunted Mountain, as he gathers to his side the ghosts of a people who in an earlier age had sworn to fight Sauron and then failed to honor their promise. The scene then switches again to Rohan, where King Theoden musters his people for the ride to Minas Tirith. They start on their ride, but already as the scene switches back to Minas Tirith the siege has started. The forces of Mordor have breached the outer defenses when suddenly, in a moment which redeems all the suspense, the trumpet of Rohan is heard in the distance. The battle is still in doubt, however, until Aragorn arrives with his army of ghosts, thereby tying all the strands of the plot together again.

Of course, *The Lord of the Rings* does have its weak moments. Tolkien's figures of good suffer from the same kind of abstractness that afflicts Lewis's Ares and Aphrodite. This is the same problem Tolkien had in *The Hobbit,* in presenting the positive side of life. The elf-king Elrond is a walking paradox, "ageless, neither young nor old," as is his queen, Galadriel ("Young she was and yet not so") (*FR,* 299). These phrases are typical of the abstract and self-consciously elevated writing that flows from Tolkien's pen whenever he writes of the elves. They simply don't have the same kind of immediacy that Frodo or Sam or even Sauron has.

The same can be said of Tolkien's heroic figures. Although more fully realized than Bard in *The Hobbit,* Aragorn, for instance, is still not quite convincing. Throughout the story Tolkien's thematic concerns, i.e., the sadness of political life, weigh his character down. Too often Aragorn does not *be,* but *mean.* Aragorn explains himself and his work in these terms. "Lonely men are we, Rangers of the wild, hunters—but hunters ever of the servants of the Enemy; for they are found in many places, not in Mordor only" (*FR,* 326). What is true of Aragorn is even truer of the lesser characters. They are there only for fighting. They generally have no domestic life, none of the sense of community and place which distinguishes Tolkien's descriptions of hobbit life. This is probably due to the fact that these characters are far removed from Tolkien's own experience. The people of the Shire might have been his own acquaintances. But Tolkien's knights are drawn from a very old literature (hence their highly literary speech, e.g., "Lonely men are we"), and Tolkien's attempts to breathe life into them are generally unsuccessful.

In general, however, the story is well told and the themes well developed. Although it is occasionally boring, it is unusually successful in maintaining reader interest through thirteen hundred long pages. But more than this, *The Lord of the Rings* is one of the best expressions of a whole generation's dismay at the modern world.

In conclusion, I would like to turn once more to Tolkien's essay on *Beowulf.* In describing the development of Christian poetry from *Beowulf* on, he makes a distinction between the *Beowulf* poet and later, more openly Christian writers which captures the difference between his own work and that of C.S. Lewis. Like the *Beowulf* poet, Tolkien is primarily concerned with "men under heaven" and "the great temporal defeat." On the other hand, Lewis insists that "the real battle is between the soul and its adversaries." He is much more interested in showing that there is "no defeat."

Thus although Tolkien and Lewis have very similar backgrounds (upper middle class, high Church), similar experiences (private schools, the war) and similar commitments (Christianity, the intellectual life), they respond to these experiences in different ways. For Tolkien, the experience of the war seems to have been most important. This experience left a deep pessimism about life and society, a pessimism which is reflected in much of his work but especially in his masterpiece, *The Lord of the Rings*. There, all elements of plot, character, theme, and tone combine to present a view of life which is thoroughly somber.

For Lewis, the experience of the patriarchal family and of the corrupt social life of his school sent him into a sustained search for alternative values to those of the individualistic, competitive, and materialistic society around him. Part of the answer he found in the life of a scholar. Part of it in a circle of close friends. Even more important was his espousal of Christianity, which not only rejects material striving but also promises a future refuge from a corrupt world. Finally, his reaction served as the impulse for his writing, both in its polemical and fantasy aspects. At its best, his writing takes us into worlds which center on problems of moral choice and worlds whose magic and splendour provide an imaginative refuge from the modern world.

Notes

Chapter 1

1. Quotations from the works of C.S. Lewis are cited in the text using the following abbreviations:

AL:	*The Allegory of Love* (Oxford: The Clarendon Press, 1936).
AM:	*The Abolition of Man* (London: Oxford University Press, 1944).
DP:	"The Dethronement of Power," in *Tolkien and the Critics,* edited by Neil D. Isaacs and Rose A. Zimbardo (Notre Dame, Ind.: University of Notre Dame Press, 1968).
EC:	*An Experiment in Criticism* (New York: Harcourt, Brace & World, 1961).
GM:	*George Macdonald: An Anthology,* edited by C.S. Lewis (London: G. Bles, 1946).
HB:	*The Horse and His Boy* (New York: Collier Books, 1970).
L:	*Letters of C.S. Lewis* (New York: Harcourt, Brace & World, 1966).
LB:	*The Last Battle* (New York: Collier Books, 1970).
LWW:	*The Lion, the Witch, and the Wardrobe* (New York: Collier Books, 1970).
MN:	*The Magician's Nephew* (New York: Collier Books, 1970).
OOW:	*Of Other Worlds* (New York: Harcourt, Brace, & World, 1966).
OSP:	*Out of the Silent Planet* (New York: Macmillan, 1965).
P:	*Perelandra* (New York: Macmillan, 1965).
PC:	*Prince Caspian* (New York: Collier Books, 1970).
Poems:	*Poems,* edited by Walter Hooper (London: G. Bles, 1964).
SbJ:	*Surprised by Joy* (New York: Harcourt, Brace & World, 1955).
SC:	*The Silver Chair* (New York: Collier Books, 1970).
SL:	*The Screwtape Letters* and "Screwtape Proposes a Toast" (New York: Macmillan, 1962).
THS:	*That Hideous Strength* (New York: Macmillan, 1964).
TWHF:	*Till We Have Faces* (London: G. Bles, 1965).
VDT:	*The Voyage of the Dawn Treader* (New York: Collier Books, 1970).

2. Quotations from the works of J.R.R. Tolkien are cited in the text using the following abbreviations:

BMC:	"*Beowulf:* the Monster and the Critics," in *An Anthology of Beowulf Criticism,* edited by Lewis E. Nicholson (Notre Dame, Ind.: University of Notre Dame Press, 1963).
FR:	*The Fellowship of the Ring* (New York: Ballantine Books, 1965).
H:	*The Hobbit* (New York: Ballantine Books, 1965).
RK:	*The Return of the King* (New York: Ballantine Books, 1965).
TR:	*The Tolkien Reader* (New York: Ballantine Books, 1966).
TT:	*The Two Towers* (New York: Ballantine Books, 1965).

Chapter 2

1. Chad Walsh, "C.S. Lewis: The Man and the Mystery," in *Shadows of Imagination*, edited by Mark R. Hillegas (Carbondale, Ill.: Southern Illinois University Press, 1969), p. 1.

2. Clyde S. Kilby, *The Christian World of C.S. Lewis* (Grand Rapids, Mich.: Wm. B. Eerdmans, 1964), p. 13.

3. In *Light on C.S. Lewis*, edited by Joycelyn Gibb (New York: Harcourt, Brace & World, 1965), p. 24.

4. Joy Davidman, "The Longest Way Round," in *These Found the Way*, edited by D.W. Soper (Philadelphia: Westminster Press, 1951), p. 24.

5. What is even more interesting about this narrative is that Joy Davidman later married Lewis. Sometime after the composition of this narrative (as Clyde Kilby notes), Gresham began to drink again, and finally she divorced him. Afterward she went to England where she became Lewis's secretary. In 1956 she became Mrs. Lewis.

6. Nevill Coghill, "The Approach to English," in *Light on C.S. Lewis*, p. 60.

7. Walsh, "C.S. Lewis: the Man and the Mystery," p. 11.

8. Owen Barfield, in *Light on C.S. Lewis*, pp. xi, xii.

9. Ibid., p. xiv.

10. Walsh, "C.S. Lewis: the Man and the Mystery," p. 3. In his introduction to *The Pilgrim's Regress*, Lewis defines the important term "Romanticism": "What I meant was a particular recurrent experience which dominated my childhood and adolescence and which I hastily called 'Romantic' because inanimate nature and marvellous literature were among the things that evoked it.... The experience is one of intense longing" (p. 7). Lewis goes on to say that it is distinguished from other desires by two things: (1) though it is painfully intense, it is desirable in itself, and (2) the object of the desire is a mystery.

11. Richard B. Cunningham, *C.S. Lewis, Defender of the Faith* (Philadelphia: Westminster Press, 1967), p. 141.

12. See Clyde Kilby's *The Christian World of C.S. Lewis* for a survey of Lewis criticism.

13. "Tutor and Scholar," in *Light on C.S. Lewis*, p. 83.

14. *Light on C.S. Lewis*, p. 76.

15. Chad Walsh, *C.S. Lewis: Apostle to Skeptics* (New York: Macmillan, 1949), p. 57.

16. Ibid., p. 59.

17. *Light on C.S. Lewis*, p. 82.

18. Ibid., p. 83.

19. Walsh, "C.S. Lewis: the Man and the Mystery," p. 12.

Chapter 3

1. Clyde S. Kilby, *The Christian World of C.S. Lewis* (Grand Rapids, Mich.: Wm. B. Eerdmans, 1964), p. 37. I have neglected to mention Lewis's first fantasy, *The Pilgrim's Regress*, because it is Lewis's weakest work and of interest only to specialists. Basically, it

traces the escape of the author-surrogate, John, from his home in Puritania. He becomes involved in all the intellectual trends which had attracted Lewis. Finally he rejects them all and returns home determined to battle them with all his might. There are interesting moments, of course, as there are in all of Lewis's writing, especially in the first chapter which describes John's alienation from Puritania, its witch-doctor clergy (who wear frightening masks), and its God, the Landlord, who "was quite extraordinarily good and kind to his tenants, and would certainly torture them to death the moment he had the slightest pretext." Mainly, however, we see the new Christian testing his polemical muscles. Lewis himself has said that the work is obscure and unfair in many of its arguments.

2. Chad Walsh, *C.S. Lewis: Apostle to the Skeptics* (New York: Macmillan, 1949), p. 51.

3. Kilby, *The Christian World of C.S. Lewis*, p. 79.

4. Ibid.

5. Ibid.

Chapter 4

1. Chad Walsh, *C.S. Lewis: Apostle to Skeptics* (New York: Macmillan, 1949), p. 160.

Chapter 5

1. Quoted in Lin Carter, *Tolkien* (New York: Ballantine Books, 1969), p. 4.

2. Ibid., p. 5.

3. William Ready, *Understanding Tolkien and the Lord of the Rings* (New York: Paperback Library, 1969), p. 57.

4. Carter, *Tolkien*, p. 8.

5. Ready, *Understanding Tolkien*, p. 11.

Chapter 6

1. Lin Carter, *Tolkien* (New York: Ballantine Books, 1969), p. 11.

Chapter 7

1. Mark Robert Hillegas ed., *Shadows of Imagination* (Carbondale, Ill.: Southern Illinois University Press, 1969), p. 110.

Bibliography

Carter, Lin. *Tolkien: a Look Behind the Lord of the Rings*. New York: Ballantine Books, 1969.

Cunningham, Richard B. *C.S. Lewis, Defender of the Faith*. Philadelphia: Westminster Press, 1967.

Davidman, Joy. "The Longest Way Round." *These Found the Way; Thirteen Converts to Protestant Christianity*. Edited by D.W. Soper. Philadelphia: Westminster Press, 1951.

Gibb, Joycelyn, ed. *Light on C.S. Lewis*. New York: Harcourt, Brace & World, 1965.

Hillegas, Mark Robert, ed. *Shadows of Imagination*. Carbondale, Ill.: Southern Illinois University Press, 1969.

Isaacs, Neil D., and Zimbardo, Rose A. *Tolkien and the Critics*. Notre Dame, Ind.: University of Notre Dame Press, 1968.

Kilby, Clyde S. *The Christian World of C.S. Lewis*. Grand Rapids, Mich.: W.S. Eerdmans, 1964.

Lewis, C.S. *The Abolition of Man*. London: Oxford University Press, 1944.

_____. *The Allegory of Love: A Study in Medieval Tradition*. Oxford: The Clarendon Press, 1936.

_____. *An Experiment in Criticism*. New York: Harcourt, Brace & World, 1961.

_____. *The Horse and His Boy*. New York: Collier Books, 1970.

_____. *The Last Battle*. New York: Collier Books, 1970.

_____. *Letters*. Edited with a memoir by W.H. Lewis. New York: Harcourt, Brace & World, 1966.

_____. *The Lion, the Witch, and the Wardrobe*. New York: Collier Books, 1970.

_____. *The Magician's Nephew*. New York: Collier Books, 1970.

_____. *Of Other Worlds*. Edited by Walter Hooper. New York: Harcourt, Brace, & World, 1966.

_____. *Out of the Silent Planet*. New York: Macmillan, 1965.

_____. *Perelandra*. New York: Macmillan, 1965.

_____. *The Pilgrim's Regress, an Allegorical Apology for Christianity, Reason, and Romanticism*. New York: Sheed and Ward, 1935.

_____. *Poems*. Edited by Walter Hooper. London: G. Bles, 1964.

_____. *Prince Caspian*. New York: Collier Books, 1970.

_____. *The Screwtape Letters* and "Screwtape Proposes a Toast." New York: Macmillan, 1962.

_____. *The Silver Chair*. New York: Collier Books, 1970.

_____. *Surprised by Joy: The Shape of My Early Life*. New York: Harcourt, Brace & World, 1956.

_____. *That Hideous Strength*. New York: Macmillan, 1964.

_____. *Till We Have Faces*. London: G. Bles, 1965.

_____. *The Voyage of the Dawn Treader*. New York: Collier Books, 1970.

Macdonald, George. *George Macdonald: An Anthology*. Edited by C.S. Lewis. London: G. Bles, 1946.

Nicholson, Lewis E., ed. *An Anthology of Beowulf Criticism*. Notre Dame, Ind.: University of Notre Dame Press, 1963.

Ready, William. *Understanding Tolkien and the Lord of the Rings.* New York: Paperback Library, 1969.

Tolkien, J.R.R. *The Fellowship of the Ring.* New York: Ballantine Books, 1965.

_____. *The Hobbit.* New York: Ballantine Books, 1965.

_____. *The Return of the King.* New York: Ballantine Books, 1965.

_____. *The Tolkien Reader.* New York: Ballantine Books, 1966.

_____. *The Two Towers.* New York: Ballantine Books, 1965.

Walsh, Chad. *C.S. Lewis: Apostle to the Skeptics.* New York: Macmillan, 1949.

Index